Praise for *Men at Work*

"In the energy industry, where safety, performance, and innovation are non-negotiable, strong and inclusive leadership is essential. *Men at Work* offers a clear, actionable blueprint for how men in leadership can foster stronger teams and a more effective workplace culture. This book is a timely and practical guide for any leader focused on building a high-performing, future-ready organization."

—Mike Wirth, Chairman and CEO, Chevron Corporation

"Jennifer McCollum delivers a compelling framework for gender partnership that links directly to organizational performance. Her call to engage men and women as a united force for change is as refreshing as it is essential."

—Jon R. Moeller, Executive Chairman, Procter & Gamble

"*Men at Work* is a courageous and compassionate book. It reminds us that equity is not just a women's issue, but critical to our collective prosperity."

—Hillary Rodham Clinton, former First Lady,
US Senator, and Secretary of State

"In health care, equity isn't just a value; it's a vital driver of better outcomes for patients and communities alike. This essential book brings both urgency and clarity to the role men can play in advancing inclusive leadership. Jennifer McCollum delivers an enlightening message: Equity is not a solo act, but a strategic partnership."

—Paul Hudson, CEO, Sanofi

"Partnership, inclusion, and equity aren't just ideals; they're the foundation of stronger teams and better results. Sports teach us that true progress happens when every voice is valued and every talent has room to shine—and *Men at Work* provides a clear roadmap to building workplaces where that progress is possible."

—Cathy Engelbert, Commissioner, WNBA, and retired CEO, Deloitte

"*Men at Work* is a compelling call to action for leaders who believe that inclusion is both a value creator and a business imperative. Jennifer McCollum's insights resonate deeply with our experience at Dow, where trust, transparency, empowerment, and accountability have become the foundation of our culture. This book offers a practical roadmap for building workplaces where everyone has an equal opportunity to contribute, grow, and thrive."

—Jim Fitterling, Chair and CEO, Dow Inc.

"Catalyst challenges readers to move beyond allyship and embrace accountability as the path to progress. Her message is both urgent and hopeful: When men and women lead together, we all rise. This book belongs in the hands of every leader who believes in the power of partnership and inclusion."

  —Darryl White, Chief Executive Officer, BMO Financial Group

"Jennifer McCollum bridges the gap between aspiration and action. With clarity and compassion, she shows how gender partnership can transform not only our workplaces but also our culture for men and women alike. An instant classic."

  —Kenji Yoshino, Chief Justice Earl Warren Professor of Constitutional Law, NYU School of Law, and Author, *How Equality Wins*

"To create a Great Place to Work for All in the dawn of the AI era, we need to include everyone. I think Catalyst has created the most innovative partnership roadmap for these complex times."

  —Michael C. Bush, Global CEO, Great Place to Work

"In a moment when equity and inclusion are being called into question and too many leaders are retreating from the necessary march toward just workplaces, *Men at Work* affirms the urgency. From a zero-sum discussion which too often prevails, McCollum provides a roadmap for engaging men as partners and beneficiaries in building the inclusive, caring, and diverse workplaces we all need."

  —Gary Barker, PhD, CEO and Founder, Equimundo

"Great leadership is about women and men implementing Our Working Together© Leadership and Management system to create value and growth for all of the stakeholders and the greater good. In *Men at Work*, Jennifer McCollum shows how gender partnership is not only the right thing to do; it's the smart thing to do to create workplaces that deliver the best outcomes for all. Jennifer's insights will inspire leaders at every level!"

  —Alan Mulally, former CEO, Ford Motor Company and Boeing Commercial Airplanes, and former Board Director, Google (now Alphabet), Carbon 3D, and the Mayo Clinic

"*Men at Work* is a practical guide for business leaders on how we can better foster inclusiveness for everyone in the workplace. This insightful book would be helpful to those committed to cultivating an attractive talent model and building a more resilient business."

  —Karyn Twaronite, Global Vice Chair, EY, and Board of Advisors Member, Catalyst

"*Men at Work* is a compelling call to action for men in leadership. Jennifer McCollum reveals how mutual accountability—beyond simple allyship—can create lasting change. With stories that inspire and strategies you can act on today, this book is as motivating as it is practical."
—David Smith, Coauthor, *Good Guys*, and Professor and Co-Director of the Gender & Work Initiative, Johns Hopkins Carey Business School

"*Men at Work* is a powerful call to action. It shows how gender partnership strengthens families, workplaces, and communities."
—David S. Taylor, retired CEO and Chairman, Procter & Gamble, and Chairman, Delta Airlines

"Jennifer McCollum understands that leadership is a team sport. *Men at Work* is a brilliant guide to building trust, elevating others, and creating workplaces where everyone thrives. Her message is bold, actionable, and long overdue."
—Mark Thompson, Thinkers50 Coaching Legend, *New York Times* Bestselling Author, and author of newly released *CEO Ready* with Harvard Business Review

"Jennifer McCollum has written a book that every leader should read. *Men at Work* is a master class in inclusive leadership: practical, research-based, and deeply human. It challenges us to lead not just with our minds but with our hearts. This is the kind of leadership the world needs now."
—Dr. Marshall Goldsmith, *Thinkers50* #1 Executive Coach and *New York Times* Bestselling Author, *The Earned Life*, *Triggers*, and *What Got You Here Won't Get You There*

MEN
AT
WORK

Also by Jennifer McCollum

*In Her Own Voice: A Woman's Rise to CEO—Overcoming Hurdles
to Change the Face of Leadership*

MEN
AT
The Roadmap
to Gender
Partnership
WORK

JENNIFER McCOLLUM

Matt Holt Books
An Imprint of BenBella Books, Inc.
Dallas, TX

Men at Work copyright © 2026 by Catalyst Inc.

Matt Holt is an imprint of BenBella Books, Inc.
8080 N. Central Expressway
Suite 1700
Dallas, TX 75206
benbellabooks.com
Send feedback to feedback@benbellabooks.com

BenBella and *Matt Holt* are federally registered trademarks.

Printed in the United States of America
10 9 8 7 6 5 4 3 2 1

Library of Congress Control Number: 2025038650
ISBN 9781637748077 (hardcover)
ISBN 9781637748084 (electronic)

Editing by Lisa K. Marietta
Copyediting by Lynne Curry
Proofreading by Michael Fedison and Sarah Vostok
Indexing by Debra Bowman
Text design and composition by PerfecType, Nashville, TN
Cover design by Brigid Pearson
Printed by Lake Book Manufacturing

*To the Catalyst staff, boards of directors and advisors,
and our 500+ supporter organizations across more than
six decades: You have been fierce and committed advocates for
change, guiding and lifting our mission to accelerate progress
for women in the workplace through workplace inclusion.*

When workplaces work for women, they work for everyone.

CONTENTS

FOREWORD

Throughout my 31 years at Dow, I have always strived for excellence—for myself, for the organizations I supported, and for the company as a whole. This was never a solitary journey. Always, colleagues, mentors, and sponsors traveled that road with me. Partners. And as I grew, I realized the importance of playing the same role with others.

Over time, I discovered that partnership is not about building unfair advantages. It is about building out opportunities. It is not about pointing fingers. It's about pointing to a better way. It's not about keeping score. It's about scoring wins together. The power of partnership brings out the best in us, individually and collectively.

We see in *Men at Work: The Roadmap to Gender Partnership* that too often, in too many settings, true, productive partnership has not existed between men and women. This timely book acknowledges age-old behaviors and mindsets, then unpacks many as detrimental to our joint success. Through gender partnership, accountability for change and action is shared by all, but so are the benefits.

Employing rigorous research, statistics, and stories of male and female leaders, Catalyst CEO Jennifer McCollum offers a roadmap for how to build inclusion in your workplace and deliver stronger business results through true partnership. She shows how rigid stereotypes—like the idea that men must be tough, competitive, and unemotional and women cannot be assertive, ambitious, or display emotion—hold back everyone, men and women alike.

What does gender partnership look like? It looks like empathy. It looks like advocacy. It looks like action. Empathy because we must understand each other so that we can help people achieve their best. Advocacy because we must step forward and enter the arena to help ensure all colleagues have an equal opportunity to advance. Action because as women and men, we must recognize our own biases and have the courage to change, to support the larger cause, the greater mission, the collective purpose.

I have been fortunate to work for a company that values gender partnership. In fact, two of my colleagues share their stories throughout *Men at Work*—Jim Fitterling, Dow's chair and CEO, and Amy Wilson, our general counsel and corporate secretary. Their partnerships have been invaluable to me and have enriched not only my experience at Dow but also my life. Jim and I, in particular, have worked together throughout my career. He has been both mentor and sponsor advocating for me in rooms that I wasn't yet in. And over the years, I have benefitted from his counsel and guidance, even as he has urged me to find my own way.

I have been privileged to be involved with Catalyst for nearly a decade. It is an iconic organization that has effectively addressed gender opportunities and issues in the workplace since the 1960s. Its long-term impact is why I am proud to be chair of the Catalyst Advisory Board and why we are working side-by-side with Jennifer to drive success for the organization and the companies it represents.

One of Catalyst's seminal programs featured in *Men at Work* is MARC (Mutual Accountability, Real Change), and it has transformed both men and women throughout Dow. These sessions provide a safe space to react, to reflect, and to resolve to make changes. They get at the root of behaviors that we've learned over time, men and women, and biases that we have developed that are unfounded by fact. MARC has altered the way we work, and the way we work together.

Men at Work is a tremendous addition to Catalyst's contributions to strengthening the workplace. It is relevant to all of us, whether we are at a global corporation or a small nonprofit. It resonated with me at a deep, personal level because my own professional journey is a testament to the power of gender partnership. As a woman, and a woman of color, I entered an industry where often I was the first and only. As I look back over these 31 years, it is through partnerships with men and women that I have arrived at this point in my career. It is not only a tremendous honor but a real obligation to do what I can to pay it forward as a partner to others.

So much is at stake. I aim to leave my granddaughters and grandson the legacy of workplaces that are more inclusive than those my coworkers and I joined. That will require change on a global scale. It may be an enormous task, but I am keenly aware that one day the next generation will be talking about what we did or did not do in this moment—a moment where progress may seem elusive, but progress is imperative.

Therefore, my hope is that as you read this roadmap for gender partnership that you learn from Catalyst's world-renowned research, that you are inspired by the stories throughout, and most importantly, that you feel compelled to act. Partnership galvanizes, catalyzes and catapults us forward to achieve our collective goals, and could be the very thing that solves some of the world's greatest challenges.

Let's move forward together, as partners, advancing progress and accelerating real change.

Karen S. Carter
Chief Operating Officer, Dow
Chair, Catalyst Board of Advisors

INTRODUCTION

Many men have fantasies at work.

They fantasize about taking several months of parental leave when their child is born or adopted. They dream about talking openly with colleagues about the challenges of caring for aging parents and the flexibility to leave early on occasion to address personal needs. And they long for the day when they can be brutally honest about the challenges they face—such as depression, divorce, or the death of a loved one—even if it means shedding tears and being vulnerable in front of their manager and team.

Yet too many men can't fulfill these dreams because they fear doing so would make them appear weak or ineffective. It might even disqualify them for a promotion. Sadly, in many cases, they are right, and many feel alone and unfulfilled.

Research from Catalyst, the global nonprofit I lead that supports companies to accelerate progress for women by building workplaces that work for everyone, confirms that men who deviate from masculine stereotypes at work face consequences. As a result, an alarmingly high 94% of men reported to us that, at work, they have experienced at least some level of masculine anxiety—a sense of distress for not living up to traditional male expectations.[1]

Women, like men, also have fantasies. They imagine what their lives would look like if they were paid the same or promoted as quickly as their male peers in similar roles and with similar qualifications and performance. They wish for more experiences where they are supported by their colleagues and publicly acknowledged and valued for their contributions. And they want to fully embrace their authenticity instead of hiding parts of themselves to better "fit in" with the status quo or the leadership majority, which remains nearly 70% men at senior levels globally.[2]

Many women feel stuck, exhausted, and discouraged.

Believe it or not, these scenarios are two sides of the same coin: stereotypical gender roles. These constricting stereotypes are strangling many workplaces—including, very likely, your own.

Societal norms and expectations dictating how men and women are supposed to look, behave, and live their lives are harmful to everyone. For example: "Men are competitive, aggressive, and stoic. Women are cooperative, warm, and vulnerable."[3] We all know these traits are not across-the-board truths. Individual men and women are just that—individual. When we expect and even pressure people to conform to these stereotypes, we prevent them from being fully themselves. And because no one can do their best work under such circumstances—or in many cases advance to a role where they can deploy their full range of talents—organizational performance flounders.*

The solution that benefits all is to transform your workplace culture by engaging men. Why men? Because they still hold most of the

---

* At Catalyst, we fully acknowledge, respect, and honor the vast array of differences on the gender spectrum. We support people in the workplace expressing their gender in the way that feels most natural and comfortable to them. In this book we have chosen to use traditional male and female terminology: men, women, he, she, his, and hers. Please know that this decision was made only for clarity and simplicity and is not meant to exclude anyone of any gender.

leadership roles at senior levels and therefore are uniquely positioned to have a real impact on making their workplace cultures fair and more inclusive. Instead of calling them out, we need to invite them in as partners to embrace new, more flexible norms across gender. Essentially, it's about allowing—and encouraging—men and women to be themselves and freely tap into all the things that make them human, not just the parts society defines as sufficiently, stereotypically "manly" or "womanly."[4]

At Catalyst, we believe that when people at work challenge traditional expectations around masculinity by exhibiting vulnerability, empathy, flexibility, and emotional transparency; when they act as if it is "normal" for women to be ambitious and aggressively reach for high-level leadership roles; and when they advocate for equitable sharing of domestic responsibilities at home and at work, employees at all levels across gender reap the rewards. And, not incidentally, companies benefit from increased employee productivity, innovation, and commitment to stay.[5]

I am going to share a story here to show you how this plays out in the real world. Tedrick (Ted) Johnson, an executive I have always admired, has had a long and successful career at a massive health care system. He is an excellent talent spotter and speaks with pride about his team, which includes a number of women executives. Yet, he doesn't necessarily think of himself as a champion of gender equity. He will flat-out tell you that he hires the best person for the job. What he may not know, and what I certainly believe, is that his matter-of-fact approach to hiring the best person for the job inevitably results in bringing highly qualified women onto his team—and that this approach is precisely what makes him a gender partner. Talent comes in all forms. It's the people who create space for that talent to rise without barriers who make all the difference.

So back to the story: Ted has recruited four women to his leadership team in the last couple of years. He told me about bringing in a new woman executive from outside the company, which was unusual, as they rarely hire externally for these senior positions. She was the first woman to hold this role, replacing a beloved male legend, and Ted knew she was the disruptor he needed, someone with a different view of the world. At a dinner meeting where he was introducing her to some critical stakeholders, all men, Ted noticed they were addressing him directly with their ideas and questions, instead of their new executive. Finally, Ted said, "Gentlemen, I'm willing to answer whatever questions you have; but keep in mind, I am not going to be part of your day-to-day. If you really want to make things happen, you will need to go to her directly."

Traditionally, men have viewed other men as the "final authority" in the workplace. That's most likely why Ted's team was deferring to him. By letting them know that the new executive was the one in charge, Ted was sending the message that he is a leader who rejects outdated gender roles, and he expects his colleagues to do the same. He was also practicing inclusion and giving her the power and permission to be the leader she was hired to be. That is what being a gender partner looks like, even if you wouldn't naturally call yourself that or even think of yourself in those terms.

At this point, you may be asking why I, as the CEO of an organization whose mission is to help make workplaces work for women, have written this book about men. The short answer is that, at Catalyst, we recognize that when it comes to making workplaces diverse, fair, and inclusive, everyone needs to be involved.

WHO THIS BOOK IS FOR

This book is written primarily for people in leadership roles at organizations of any size who are seeking guidance on creating a more fair, inclusive workplace culture for women—while at the same time addressing the equally pressing needs of men. Men in senior corporate positions, particularly those who are white, may appreciate the roadmap and stories in this book because, until now, they largely have been excluded from conversations about workplace equity and inclusion. Additionally, they have unique perspective and power that positions them to lead the way in changing their company's workplace culture. And for women who may have never considered the toll that traditional masculine norms have on men, this book is for you too. We can all be better gender partners to each other.

For too long, men have felt left out of conversations about women's representation and ascension in the workplace. As a result, they have felt undervalued, sidelined, or even blamed for the status quo. After all, conversations about "gender" are typically understood to be about "women," and all but ignore the challenges men face in the workplace as well.

What if we could both accelerate progress for women at work *and* enable men to embrace an alternate (and healthier) vision of masculinity, emphasizing that men's strengths lie as well in their ability to be empathetic and inclusive—qualities traditionally coded as feminine? After all, the men we've talked to have overwhelmingly expressed a desire to show up this way, and they tell us that the current standards of masculinity are not working for them.

"I [bought into the idea of] being a hypermasculine guy for a very, very long time," shared Hunter Johnson, founder and CEO of The Man Cave, a preventative mental health program for teenage boys in Australia. His story exemplifies the difficulties men face in understanding and living with society's expectations of masculinity.

At a Catalyst event, Johnson revealed that, growing up, he "molded" his identity "on how good I was at sport, how much money I thought I was going to make, how many young women I thought I could attract, and if I could show as little emotion as possible doing those things." Primed to become a professional rugby player, at age 16 he suffered a life-threatening injury. For the first time, he felt vulnerable. "And that wasn't necessarily a word that was in my vocabulary as a young Australian man, but it provided an opportunity for me to question my social structure, my identity, who my role models were, and created a path where I got to think about what was really important to me."

Johnson's grandfather said to him, "If you were that good at sport, imagine if you could push that into something a little more meaningful?"

That observation was transformative for Johnson. "It opened up this whole world of social change and impact. I had been seeing men in my life—men who had raised me—go through anxiety, depression, and even suicide. And some of the most important women in my life started to share their stories of abuse and harassment. It just didn't make sense to me that we weren't doing something at a preventative level."[6]

This insight was also life-changing for tens of thousands of boys in Australia. The Man Cave enables boys to explore their humanity and gives them space to talk about their emotions, modeling a respectful masculinity that draws attention to men's role in equality for women, and healthy ways of being for everyone.

Giving boys and men permission to show all their facets will come as a huge relief to many, and as they grow and enter the workforce, their work lives and personal lives can be richer and more fulfilling. Too many men are exhausted, boxed in, and disconnected from their fullest selves. The same system that disadvantages women also robs men of the chance to lead with humanity, parent without stigma, admit fear, or feel whole.

The beauty of this strategy is that it helps women too. And women definitely need help. Progress for women in the workplace has stalled, with women continuing to lag in pay equity and leadership representation.[7] Many organizations are failing to attract, retain, and advance women—putting their companies at risk of a talent gap, under-representation of women at senior levels, weaker employee productivity and innovation, and the appearance that advancing women is not a core company value.[8]

Women employees in such companies are likely burned out and seeking better options with your competitors, and talented prospects are looking elsewhere. This is especially true for our youngest generations, who value workplace diversity, equity, and inclusion initiatives and factor them into their employment decisions.[9] Failure to meet people where they are and to give them what they want in the workplace can undermine a company's viability in our rapidly shifting world.

If we want to change the status quo, we need to disrupt the old way of doing things, especially the way we think about gender for men *and* for women.

Men at Work offers guidance and tools to create culture change. I draw from original Catalyst research and data along with other significant research, brought to life with personal stories of exceptional men and the organizations they help lead. The evidence demonstrates that we can't advance women without the participation of men as mutually accountable partners. And when we do so, men benefit too.

It's time for a new roadmap. And this book will guide you and your company to a better destination.

Men Want to Advance Women in the Workplace; Let's Help Them

The way men and women work together matters more than ever, not just from a "moral" standpoint but also from a performance one. Most men in the workplace (like most women) understand and care about both.

Women make up nearly half the workforce in the United States but fewer than 10% of CEO roles in the S&P 500 and 29% of senior vice president positions in companies across North America.[10] In most companies globally, this data is worse, and it's impacting the organizations' ability to drive the innovation and collaboration needed to succeed in the marketplace.

Building bridges between men and women creates better performance outcomes and better places to work. It engages people, builds job satisfaction and trust, and fosters the feelings of belonging and well-being that today's employees value. All of this sets up companies to attract the best and the brightest and convince them to stay.

The solution is twofold. One, we need to educate men and women on how traditional gender norms and roles can be harmful to them and to healthy workplace dynamics. Two, we need to equip and support them around *how* to work both within and across lines of gender in ways that enable teamwork, build strong relationships, and accelerate performance.

Our latest research with over 5,000 men from 9 countries and more than 12 industries shows that **the overwhelming majority of men *do* want to close gender gaps at work**. In fact, almost all men want organizations to take action to ensure that outcomes for employees across genders are fair and the different barriers and advantages that each person experiences are recognized. For example, 76% of men want their organization to identify areas where women employees are disadvantaged and change the culture in ways that produce gender equity.[11] The good news is that when people know better, they do better. We at Catalyst have seen this truth play out again and again. That's why I wrote this book. We wanted to offer a research-based, commonsense approach to reshaping gender norms and roles in the workplace and creating cultures where *everyone* can thrive. Engaging men in this way is not just the right thing to do; it's a business imperative. The message is clear: If you want to help men in your organization to advance and thrive in their careers while also enabling women in your organization to do the same, you must make the workplace inclusive for everyone—including men.

Why Focus on Men?

As we touched on earlier, men themselves are struggling against traditional gender norms in ways that have historically gone unacknowledged and unnoticed. Thankfully, we at Catalyst have been researching and offering solutions on this topic for over a decade. Now, more people are recognizing and talking about the problems men face in our culture, and awareness is building.

For example, millions of American men are lonely, with 15% *reporting they have no close friends.*[12] In a 2023 survey of men age 18 to 45, *most agreed that "no one really knows me well."*[13] In fact, one in five men in the United States experiences depression, yet men are less likely than women to seek treatment,[14] and the global suicide rate for men is more than double that of women, according to the World Health Organization,[15] and in the US specifically, nearly four times that of women, according to the Centers for Disease Control.[16] But many men suffer alone, including at work.

In the workplace, men tell us, they feel singled out, blamed, and shamed because of their identity. With attention and efforts often focused on advancing women and other underrepresented groups, they feel excluded and even targeted. After all, during most conversations about fairness and inclusion at work, the focus is on specific elements of gender, race, and sexual orientation. Men—heterosexual white men specifically—are rarely the subject, exacerbating their sense that they aren't a welcome part of the conversations and don't know how to engage, even if they want to.

Simultaneously, many workplaces have a culture favoring stereotypical norms—that men should always and only be tough, unemotional, and competitive.

The result? Men are often unable to experience the sense of inclusion and belonging that everyone deserves, nor are they able to see their role in the solution to create healthy work environments.

The Catalyst solution is to invite men to the conversation. By helping advance women, they help their company be more successful, which also benefits them. (The adage about the rising tide lifting all boats comes to mind here.) But also, a critical outcome of this work is that it also gives men tacit permission to step outside of rigid gender roles and be more of their authentic selves.

Frankly, we need men as partners. We can't continue the progress for women in the workplace without them. To quote research from the Boston Consulting Group, 96% of companies surveyed globally reported progress in achieving equality for women when men were engaged in gender diversity efforts. Only 30% of companies showed progress when men were not involved.[17]

That's where Catalyst comes in. We've looked at what is preventing men from being part of the solution, and there are real barriers, at the individual level—like apathy, ignorance, and fear—and at the organizational level, with cultures that encourage or reward keeping men in traditional gender roles.[18] We believe we can change that.

Engaging Men as Part of the Solution

Catalyst invites men to the table, together with colleagues across gender, through our MARC® (Mutual Accountability, Real Change) initiative, which inspires employees at all levels to leverage their unique opportunity and responsibility to be advocates for fair and inclusive progress, so everyone benefits. Underpinned by Catalyst's landmark research, originating in 2009, on men's barriers to engaging in gender-focused organizational initiatives, this set of experiential learning programs started in 2016 and originally focused on *male allyship* of women. But more recently, based on new understanding through our research and the experiences of thousands of leaders at all levels, we have evolved our focus toward enhancing *gender partnership*. I experienced MARC myself in the summer of 2024 for the first time and found it transformational for the nearly 40 executives who all developed a deeper awareness and understanding of the challenges both women and men face. We came away with practical tools, techniques, and language that we can use in our day-to-day work.

One recent anecdote is characteristic of the feedback we get. A male participant in our MARC program for managers shared that he has three kids—a son and two daughters. When he coaches their soccer games, he says, "I tell my son to go out there and play his hardest and win, and I tell my daughters to go out there and have fun. And now I realize that I have been inadvertently demonstrating unconscious bias and gender-role stereotyping." These "aha!" moments that occur during MARC workshops enable men to not only be better colleagues and managers at work; they also equip them to be better parents, spouses, and friends.

Let me add that while the primary focus of MARC was originally about engaging men, it has never been exclusive to men. That said, we deliberately include a focus on men because the work of building workplaces and societies where *everyone* can thrive will not succeed without them. MARC is about effective partnership; it aims to bring together men and women so they can assume mutual accountability to accelerate progress on inclusion and work together to achieve collective culture change.

Catalyst research, which we will dive into in this book, shows that most men fear repercussions if they support women's advancement and gender equity in their workplace.[19] For this reason, it's essential that organizations build climates that not only value and reward inclusion for everyone but also enable employees to speak up without fear of backlash.

What Is Gender Partnership?

We call our invitation to men "gender partnership." This ethic of collaboration is foundational to our MARC initiative. A *gender partner* is someone of any gender who assumes mutual accountability for advancing gender equity and inclusion and works collectively to advance culture change for the benefit of everyone. Put simply, a gender partner is anyone who:

1. believes it's their role to build a more fair and inclusive environment;
2. engages in that work alongside partners regardless of gender; and
3. works toward outcomes that benefit everyone.

Through gender partnership, men can reorient their relationship to their own masculinity, which can have a profound effect on the workplace in a way that serves everyone. And women can gain a deeper understanding of the challenges men face in the workplace as well.[20]

Catalyst's Vice President of Solution Development, Alix Pollack, who birthed the concept of "gender partnership," has emerged as a leading voice in this space. She shares an incident that demonstrates what gender partnership looks like. Several years ago, when she was head of the MARC program, she arrived at a training program she was facilitating. The on-site contact for the client had not met her before. In fact, she'd only been told to expect someone named "Alex." The contact person approached Alix and said, "Let me know when Alex gets here." Alix shared that *she,* in fact, was the person the contact was looking for. Later, Alix reflected on the moment:

> Yet even after I said that Alix was me, she continued asking me housekeeping questions—"When should we tell the caterer to expect us to break for lunch?" "How many markers would we need?" And she directed all content-related questions to my co-facilitator, a man who was a junior colleague.
>
> My colleague noticed the dynamic playing out—that he, not I, was the default person in charge. He grabbed a stack of workbooks and began laying them out so that I could focus my attention on readying the session with the client. The client, however, continued to address her substantive questions exclusively to my colleague.
>
> My colleague behaved as a true gender partner does: He kept his eyes on me to show, through his body language, that I was the one in charge. After a few moments, the directional energy of the conversation shifted, and the client started looking to me for answers.

Alix notes that what made her colleague's behavior a beautiful example of gender partnership was that it didn't involve making an overt statement like, "Hey, you shouldn't assume that just because I'm a man, I'm the one in charge!" Similar to Ted earlier in this chapter, Alix's colleague did not get on a soapbox and make a proclamation about feminism or gender roles.

"Gender partnership," Alix adds, "is simply about being there for each other. Sometimes you do have to be more vocal or visible, and that kind of gesture has its place, but gender partnership is not about 'saving' women. It's about co-creating a dynamic of fairness and respect."

The Catalyst Roadmap: 5 B's of Gender Partnership

In the second half of the book, you will find the tools for gender partnership, which at Catalyst we call the 5 B's. Here's a quick synopsis:

1. **Begin with You**
   Being a gender partner is not something you can do without having some skin in the game. I encourage you to start with reflection so when the time comes, you are primed to use your voice and influence to make change.

2. **Break Down What's Not Working**
   Not everything is broken, but some things are—such as stereotypes, harmful or misguided assumptions, and outdated leadership norms that aren't serving anyone. Part of making progress is letting go of the things we need to leave behind.

3. **Build Up What's in It for Men**
   Men stand to gain a lot from greater workforce fairness and inclusion. But historically the benefits for men have not been a focal point of gender equity work, leaving many men feeling excluded and left behind. Gender partnership involves shining a light on the benefits for men so they are motivated to engage.

4. **Bridge the Gender Gaps**
   Gaps persist between women and men in pay, leadership representation, and intangibles such as recognition, safety, and engagement. Gender partners can bridge these gaps by helping to identify and remove the barriers that prevent all talent from fair systems and inclusive cultures.

5. **Bring Humanity to Work**
   Our colleagues come from different backgrounds and may have vastly different experiences and viewpoints from our own. But we are all connected by our humanity. Gender

partners bring empathy and build empowering environments
where people can bring their authenticity and lead in ways
that serve the organizations best, regardless of gender.

I don't just tell you about the 5 B's; I also show you what they look
like in practice. Successful executives shared with me how they embed
the 5 B's into their own gender partnership work, and I in turn reveal
their best practices with you. What you will find is these behaviors and
practices reflect both inner work (what Catalyst calls "leading inward"
with curiosity, humility, and courage) and interpersonal work (what
we call "leading outward," ensuring team members feel ownership,
accountability, and support). That's because gender partnership builds
off the tenets of inclusive leadership—a topic Catalyst has long been on
the leading edge of researching, promoting, and teaching.[21]

Why Listen to Catalyst?

Catalyst has a proven method of accelerating women's progress at work
by enlisting men to be part of creating positive change. It is born from
over 60 years of experience working with companies as they disrupt
and innovate for fair and inclusive workplaces. When founder and first
president Felice N. Schwartz created Catalyst in 1962, "Help Wanted"
advertisements were segregated by gender and race,[22] and the law per-
mitted companies in the United States to pay women less than men.[23]
The landscape has changed dramatically in the decades since then, and
so has Catalyst. We have grown into a global organization that helps
companies worldwide build workplaces that work for women.[24]

When Catalyst first launched, the organization was focused on helping individual women enter the workforce and stay there. We advocated
for flex-time, part-time, and job-sharing—unheard-of concepts at that
time—and participated in several early pilot programs demonstrating
that these positions were effective solutions for employers. Schwartz's

wildly popular 1972 book, *How to Go to Work When Your Husband Is Against It, Your Children Aren't Old Enough, and There's Nothing You Can Do Anyhow*, made the case that companies should hire women who had spent time out of the workplace to raise families—because women made great employees.[25]

During the 1970s, as many women in the US increasingly prepared to spend a substantial period of their lives in the workforce,[26] Catalyst created national career resource centers as well as a comprehensive library at our New York headquarters and connected women with resources offering career counseling—all part of our efforts to assist individual women getting into, or back into, the workforce. Throughout the 1970s and 1980s, we also focused our efforts on undergraduate women, encouraging thoughtful career planning and preparation.

We drove the conversation about women in corporate leadership, helping companies identify qualified women for their boards of directors. We demonstrated that there were women ready and qualified for board service, helped companies identify those women, and began to annually track the number of women on boards, publicizing when progress occurred—and when it did not.

By the late 1980s, Catalyst recognized that the obstacle women faced was not themselves—it was organizations. *The systems themselves needed real change.* In response, we made a critical shift. Rather than emphasizing what *women* could do to help themselves, we focused on what *companies* should do to create better, more women-friendly workplaces and ensure access to the highest ranks of leadership.

To that end, we began advising companies that wanted to do better. Our research, informed by our community of top global companies who supported us, refined our understanding of what works, what doesn't, and why, when it comes to creating systemic change for women. From a hard-data, bottom-line approach, we came to realize that to change organizational behavior to drive inclusion, we needed to engage both hearts and minds.

In 1989, Schwartz published "Management Women and the New Facts of Life" in the *Harvard Business Review* about the obstacles women face in the workforce. She proposed a separate track for women who planned to take extended parenting leave and desired flexibility to help balance career and family responsibilities.[27] That led to a discussion of the "mommy track." This controversial phrase was coined by the *New York Times* and not used by Schwartz. The article sparked a much-needed conversation about women's desires to have a family and career and about mothers returning to the workforce after leaving to raise children.[28]

During the 1990s, Catalyst turned its lens to the absence of women from boards and executive suites. We produced research reports showing that, in fact, many companies lacked any women at the highest levels. Notably, our research pointed to a cultural problem: persistent gender stereotypes about women in leadership roles that impede women's advancement.[29] We also deepened our understanding that women do not all share the same experiences, and we began emphasizing an intersectional approach in our research—meaning we looked not only at gender but also at how gender interacts with other dimensions of identity and experience, like race and class.

Of all our research, among our most significant was about women of color and the unique barriers they faced in US workplaces. In the late 1990s, Catalyst began collecting and reporting the number of officers and board directors who were women of color, with the data proving that they were left further behind than white women enabled us to deepen our research.[30]

We launched a groundbreaking three-year study—the first of its kind—on the barriers women of color face in their efforts to advance in the workplace, stirring a national conversation in the United States about the challenges facing Black, Latina, and Asian American women in management.[31]

Catalyst has been an early and consistent vocal advocate for inclusive workplaces. To enable all women to thrive, organizations need to create an environment of inclusion. And that environment must involve and benefit men as well.

What You Will Discover

By the time you finish reading this book, you will learn:

- Men and women alike are struggling in the workplace because of stereotypical expectations around how they are "supposed to" operate.
- Disrupting these gender norms creates work environments that benefit everyone, not just women.
- Like women, men also deserve to feel included and experience a sense of belonging, which means the freedom to break out of rigid gender roles.
- As we look to address these challenges, men have a singularly critical role in driving positive change for themselves and to advance progress for women.
- Men in leadership roles, in particular, should stand up as gender partners because as the majority, they have additional power and visibility to drive change.
- This isn't about saving or fixing women; it's also not about fixing men. It's about working together as partners to create workplaces that work for everyone.
- When men step up as agents of change for women, they benefit too.

The Catalyst approach to gender partnership enables us all to address stereotypes around "traditional masculinity" (such as applying or accepting pressure to be competitive, tough, and unemotional) and "traditional femininity" (such as applying or accepting pressure to be cooperative, collaborative, and kind) that weave into leadership norms and expectations in ways that do not serve their employees or businesses well.

If your organization has not invited men to collaborate on efforts toward women's progress or has not expanded the conversation around inclusion to be about men's experiences, too, it's not too late. The sooner you take action, the sooner you and your teams will benefit. Through creating the conditions that allow real gender partnership to flourish, we can bring men and women together to cocreate a workplace where *everyone* feels valued, *everyone* can experience belonging, and *everyone* can share in the many rewards that follow.

PART ONE
The Problem

In Part 1, I lay out the challenges that impede the powerful business imperative to create fair and inclusive workplaces where everyone—women *and* men—can thrive. Research reveals the ways in which many workplaces aren't set up to benefit either women or men. I then delve into the reasons, backed by Catalyst data, that many men—who overwhelmingly want to step up on behalf of women's advancement and create a culture in which men, too, can flourish without compromising their humanity—are held back. As you will discover, many men are impeded by fear, ignorance, and apathy. Additionally, many companies have a workplace culture that favors combative, rigid masculine norms that lead to a "climate of silence" in which employees are fearful of speaking up.

When we get it right, we build high-performing teams, fuel collaboration and innovation, create better places to work, and attract and retain the best talent. Yet even today, women continue to be left behind—in pay, representation, and opportunity. At the same time, men are also held back by workplace conditions that may box them into societal norms, inhibiting their ability to be their best. We all want to get it right, but to do so, we first need to become aware of what's not working and why.

1

Why Workplaces Don't Work for Women—and the Business Imperative for Change

Many workplaces have never been fully set up with systems or cultures that enable women to thrive. Today, to compete effectively in a dynamic and evolving marketplace, organizations face a business imperative to remove barriers that hold back any talent segment.

A healthy workplace provides opportunities for everyone: women *and* men. As we will continue to explore throughout this book, everyone wants to work in this type of environment. Why wouldn't we? A company with a healthy culture provides not only a fair income but also a sense of stability, an avenue for career and personal growth, and, frankly, a rewarding way to spend 40-plus hours a week. There's no doubt about it: Making sure women have equal opportunity to advance is simply good business. When women are in positions of leadership, companies win. The reality is that corporate boards with a critical mass of three or more women can lead to multiple benefits, such as enhanced decision-making that includes different points of view.[1] In fact, mixed-gender boards tend to have more engaged members,[2] make more sound financial decisions,[3] and are less likely to engage in controversial business practices.[4] And these benefits trickle down from the board level to have a far-reaching impact throughout the organization, with increased performance across outcomes such as work environment and values, motivation, innovation, accountability—and, yes, financial performance.

Yet, it's clear that workplaces are not working for women. And truthfully, they also aren't working for men. We'll explore men's perspective in the next chapter, but for now let's focus on women and the obstacles they face. Over the next few pages, I discuss the realities for women and how many are thwarted when they aspire to progress, in terms of both being promoted to leadership positions as well as being treated fairly and respectfully regardless of position. Naming the stumbling blocks is critical to addressing them so that we can take the next step—removing the barriers and achieving the positive outcomes transcend just business.

Workplaces Aren't Working for Women

The Likability Trap

I'll start with the likability trap because I've faced it myself. Most women have experienced the unrealistic expectations of needing to be both competent and likable in the workplace—two attributes that are often considered in opposition to each other. If a woman is well-liked, there is a higher chance that she's not regarded as competent. Yet if she's perceived as competent, there's a higher chance that she isn't well-liked.[5]

Years before the 2023 movie *Barbie*,[6] Catalyst conducted foundational research on this double-bind dilemma for women at work.[7] In the movie, America Ferrera in her role as Gloria famously delivered a speech on the myriad ways women are caught in no-win situations. The long list of expectations for women included lines like "You have to never get old, never be rude, never show off, never be selfish, never fall down, never fail, never show fear, never get out of line," and it included the zinger, "You have to be a boss, but you can't be mean."

Ferrera's monologue went viral[8] because so many women related to it personally. While men who take charge are regarded as strong, decisive, and assertive, women who behave the exact same way are often disliked. Meanwhile, when women take care, others see them as nurturing, emotional, and communicative—but lacking in competence.

As a result, women who want to succeed and advance in the workplace—and simply be treated better—must spend additional time during work hours proving they are competent leaders, again and again. They are forced to monitor, and compensate for, stereotypical perceptions of them as leaders.

It is now well understood that these gender stereotypes harm women in the workplace, which is in part why the *Barbie* movie resonated with so many people. But we can't lose sight of the fact that gender stereotypes are equal-opportunity offenders, harming men as well as women.[9] In fact, Ryan Gosling as Ken in the same movie demonstrated to a comical extreme the masculine stereotypes that portray men as one-dimensionally unemotional, aggressive, and ambitious.

Obviously, dismantling stereotypes is good for all of us in the workplace. I really related to Ferrera's speech because, early in my career, I had a formative experience that has followed me for decades. (We often hear these barriers for women called the "glass ceiling," but it really should be the plural "glass ceilings," since there are multiple obstacles that can prevent women from achieving their goals.)

I was in my mid-twenties and had landed my dream job as public relations manager at the Coca-Cola Company. My first assignment was managing the news media and branding for one of the company's most important sponsorships, the Olympic Games, which were held in Atlanta that year. Coca-Cola was sponsoring the historic Olympic Torch Relay—the magnificent migration of the Olympic flame from Athens, Greece. It was so exciting to represent Coca-Cola and oversee its media coverage of the celebratory caravan that spanned 15,000 miles over 87 days and included 10,000 local community heroes across 42 states who had been selected to serve as torchbearers. I still remember how intent I was on proving myself a worthy professional in this visible, once-in-a-lifetime role.

Unfortunately, my counterpart on the Atlanta Olympic Committee, David, saw me as a competitor rather than a collaborator, and he actively thwarted my efforts. Nevertheless, I persisted. I realized that to succeed I would have to do what women in the workplace have long been forced to: I would do whatever it took to demonstrate that I could achieve our ambitious goals—even if that meant I risked being unlikable.

So, did being unlikable work? There are two answers to this question.

Yes. After a year of relentless hard work, I achieved all the objectives of my assignment.

And also, no. Hours before the Olympic Opening Ceremonies, when the caravan with the Olympic flame stopped at the Coca-Cola headquarters, my male boss bounded over to me with congratulations and a huge smile. "You'll never believe what David just called you—it's hilarious! He said, 'Jennifer is like a cupcake with a razor blade inside.'"

Truthfully, I did not find this funny or flattering. In fact, I was devastated. It was many years later that I learned how commonly women face this double bind in the workplace, but I certainly recognized at the time that a man would never be described that way.

Of course, this experience was no anomaly. Similar attitudes have plagued women throughout modern history, especially as they secured paying jobs in much larger numbers. Women's participation began to rise in the 1930s because of increased opportunities for highly educated women.[10] Yet, as Janet Yellen, an American economist and United States secretary of the treasury (2021–2025), has pointed out, most married women were "expected to have short careers, and women were still largely viewed as secondary earners whose husbands' careers came first."[11]

In 1990, when Catalyst founder Felice Schwartz visited the Wharton School and met with members of the campus group Women at Wharton, she was shocked to learn that married women in the MBA program tended to remove their wedding bands before going to job interviews. The situation was "patently obvious to these women," Schwartz wrote in her book *Breaking with Tradition*. "Recruiters will not offer the plum jobs to those women they believe will have commitments to their families."[12] Meanwhile, men did *not* remove their wedding bands, because they knew they would be perceived as workers first, husbands and fathers second.

FLIP THE SCRIPT ON GENDER STEREOTYPES ABOUT WOMEN[13]

WHAT PEOPLE SAY: "She's a good decision maker, but she's not very nice."

WHAT TO SAY INSTEAD: "She's a good decision maker."

WHY: Research shows that when women succeed in stereotypically "masculine" areas like leadership, their success is interpreted as a sign that they lack sociability skills regarded as "feminine," like being supportive and collaborative. In other words, women are perceived as competent at the expense of being likable. This gender stereotype creates a double standard in how women are judged that can limit their opportunities for leadership and even stand in the way of their receiving basic respect.

TAKE ACTION: Question how gender stereotypes might inform how you judge women at work and the behaviors, traits, and standards you expect of them.

———

WHAT PEOPLE SAY: "Why don't you take the meeting notes? You're so helpful."

WHAT TO SAY INSTEAD: "Let's rotate taking notes and facilitating our department meetings."

WHY: When women are praised for their supportiveness, they are less likely to be thought of as leaders. Gender stereotypes about leadership can also be reinforced through subtle actions that become part of the workplace culture, such as assigning office "housework" only to women. Research shows that women, particularly women of color, are more often asked to perform these nonessential and undervalued tasks[14] and that time spent in low-promotability work can limit women's advancement opportunities.[15]

TAKE ACTION: Praise contributions to the project or team without resorting to gender stereotypes. Rotate shared tasks.

———

WHAT PEOPLE SAY: "You're being too emotional."

WHAT TO SAY INSTEAD: "I disagree but appreciate your point of view."

WHY: Women are seen as less competent and less deserving of high-status positions when they display anger,[16] and statements that disparage passionate responses reinforce the gender stereotype that women are unable to regulate their emotions and are thus less fit for leadership roles.[17] Research also suggests that when women are described in this way, their arguments are delegitimized.[18] Turning the focus away from what the woman is saying to how she's saying it is one way of dismissing her contributions, authority, and expertise.

TAKE ACTION: Question your own reactions to displays of emotion in the workplace—from people across gender—and ask whether gender and racial stereotypes are informing your perceptions.[19] Rather than focusing on the perceived emotional state of your colleague, focus on the issues being raised and keep to the topics under discussion.

The Way It Used to Be

Trailblazing changemaker Hillary Rodham Clinton—a champion of democracy and human rights for everyone—joined the 2024 Catalyst Awards Conference. In a fireside chat with former Catalyst president and CEO Lorraine Hariton, Clinton shared her candid observations on what we have accomplished as women in the workforce, and where we need to go from here.[20]

Clinton reminded us that until recently in the US, girls and women were blatantly and unapologetically treated as second-class citizens and given "a very clearly designated lane we were supposed to follow." She presented herself as a living example. In the early 1960s, when she was 14, inspired by President Kennedy, Secretary Clinton wrote a letter to the National Aeronautics and Space Administration (NASA), saying she wanted to become an astronaut and asking what she would need to do to accomplish her dream. The letter she received in response said that NASA was not interested in women.

As a young married woman in the 1970s, Clinton was not legally able to obtain a credit card in her own name. "This may seem like ancient history," she said, "but Lorraine and I both lived through it." She reminded us that Supreme Court Justice Ruth Bader Ginsburg was instrumental in knocking down many legal obstacles, as was Title IX, the 1972 landmark federal civil rights law that provided equal opportunity to girls and women in athletics and academics.

In the mid-1980s, Sam Walton, the founder of Walmart, called Clinton and asked her to serve on Walmart's board. Was it because of her qualifications? Yes and no. He told her that his wife and daughter said he needed a woman on the board. "Okay, would you be that woman?" she remembers him asking. Clinton continued, "And, of course, I was the *only* woman on the board. It was an extraordinary opportunity for me to be involved when we were beginning to recognize the role of diversity, equity, and inclusion in the corporate boardroom."

Clinton punctuated the lack of gender parity she and millions of others experienced with anecdotes about what they wore in the workplace. As the first woman partner at the Rose Law Firm in Arkansas, Clinton shared that she dressed in the same outfit that many professional women did in the 1970s and '80s—a navy blue skirt suit with a white blouse and a ribbon tied around the neck. "It was not a great look," Clinton said with a dry laugh. Yet standing out by wearing clothes that reflected her personality was simply too risky.

Many Catalyst Awards Conference attendees were familiar with the "uniform" corporate women previously wore to work and nodded ruefully along with Clinton as she spoke, but then Clinton added an anecdote that elicited gasps. One time, she heard someone tell an expert witness with short hair that she needed to go out and buy a wig with long hair if she expected to be taken seriously in the courtroom. She did.

A woman lawyer's appearance was no trivial matter; women were likely to be devalued if they deviated from feminine norms in general, and women were not even expected to be lawyers at all. "We faced what I call the 'talking dog syndrome,'" Clinton explained. "There was bewilderment that a woman could be in a courtroom trying a lawsuit."

She reminisced about an Arkansas trial at which a number of local men who were in town picking up supplies made a trip to the courtroom, filling the front row as if they were visiting a zoo. "I asked the bailiff who they were, and he said, 'They heard there was a lady lawyer in town, and they couldn't believe it and wanted to see it for themselves.'"

Some of you reading this may be well-versed in gender gaps and the driving forces behind them. For those of you who are less so or who are looking to understand how these obstacles came to be, this section is for you. As my colleague Leela Wilson, chief revenue officer, likes to say, "You can't solve a problem you don't understand."

The Pay Gap

My experience while working on the Olympics in the late 1990s, and the amazement Clinton faced as a "lady lawyer," are, by now, relics of the past, right? There's been so much attention over the last several decades to closing gender gaps in pay equity and leadership representation; surely with all this effort, women are finally getting closer to achieving parity with men.

If only it were so. In fact, the gender wage gap has *widened*, bucking the trend toward parity that had held for two decades. In 2023, men's median earnings had risen 3% while women's grew only 1.5%, according to LeanIn.org and McKinsey & Company, whose tenth anniversary report findings are based on data in the largest study of women in corporate America from more than 1,000 companies and over 480,000 employees in jobs across all levels, from entry-level to the C-suite.[21]

Based on today's wage gap, women need to work an extra eight *years* to catch up to the earnings that white, non-Hispanic men make by age 60.[22]

Broken down by race/ethnicity:

- Asian women[23] need to work an extra 2 years.
- White, non-Hispanic women[24] need to work an extra 10 years.
- Black women[25] need to work an extra 20 years.
- Native Hawaiian and other Pacific Islander women[26] need to work an extra 21 years.
- Latinas[27] need to work an extra 29 years.
- Indigenous women[28] need to work an extra 29 years.

In other words, over a lifetime career, it's as if women on average go 8 of their working years without pay—putting in between 2 to nearly 30 years of unpaid labor when compared to the earnings of their white male peers over the same time period.

"Even at this current rate of progress," according to the *Harvard Business Review*, "it will still take almost 50 years to reach parity [in pay and representation] for all women in corporate America—and that's if everything goes right, which it almost never does."[29] Particularly concerning is the fact that younger women—those under 30—face the same obstacles, such as experiences with sexual harassment and shouldering the majority of household chores at home, as those who are 50 and older.[30] It's common to assume things are getting better for women over time, but this data shows that younger women are not necessarily faring any better than those in older generations.

The Leadership Representation Gap

At the top of the corporate pyramid, women make up a declining share of global CEOs, slipping to 5.6% in 2024 from 5.8% in 2023. Women CEOs represent only 28 out of 500 companies of the world's largest businesses by revenue.[31] And this concerning gap in representation extends to all leadership levels.

Like the pay gap, this is not only bad for women—it's bad for business. For organizations to succeed and thrive, so must women.

Let me dig into the numbers for a moment to paint the picture of why women are not advancing the way they should. The pipeline of talent out of college and all higher education is majority-women,[32] and yet the labor participation gap between men and women persists— meaning that well-qualified talent is left untapped.

Nearly all (90%) women under 30 working in corporate America want to advance to the next level, and 75% aim to become senior leaders.[33] And when they do, their impact can be tremendous. EY's (previously known as Ernst & Young) research on business performance, which includes its largest client-serving groups, found that groups with a higher percentage of women partners achieved improved profitability, with a 4% higher gross margin and 10% higher total net revenue per full-time equivalent.[34] These are impressive statistics, which reinforce the business case for gender diversity at the most senior levels.

It's no wonder that talent recruitment and retention of women remain a top priority of global CEOs. And yet, while the focus may be there, the fix is not. Women leaders are exiting their corporate roles at unprecedented rates due to three main factors: wanting to advance but facing headwinds; being overworked and underrecognized; and seeking a different culture of work (e.g., flexibility, different workplace culture, etc.).[35]

By conservative estimates, each departure could cost up to two times their annual salary to replace.[36] Losing just one employee can cost a median-size S&P 500 company up to $52,000.[37] Additionally, there is not only a monetary cost but a hit to office culture as well; losing women leaders can send a message to junior women that they have less chance of advancing and therefore should leave for a better work culture elsewhere.

In sum, billions of dollars are on the line.[38]

Understanding the Why: Root Causes Behind Stalled Progress

McKinsey and LeanIn data demonstrate that women are underrepresented even at the start of their careers.[39] Catalyst found the same thing in our research from over 15 years ago,[40] evidence that some things have not changed. Even today, women are less likely than men to be hired into entry-level positions. They are then far less likely than men to be promoted to a manager role.

Our data shows that while men receive more compensation when they switch jobs, women are paid more when they stay in their jobs—an example of men being rewarded for their potential while women are compensated for their performance.[41] This means that gender stereotypes can result in very real costs for women and their organizations. Women's career progression is slowed, as they are required to spend more time accruing experiences before they are offered next-level growth compared to their male counterparts. This costs women in advancement and financial compensation, and it leaves their valuable talent untapped. This uneven approach to recognition of potential also means that organizations are disproportionately investing valuable resources in ill-timed mentoring or one-size-fits-all leadership development programs for women rather than offering them more relevant on-the-job stretch experiences they really need at key stages in their career.

Relatedly, when women understandably don't raise their hand without having 100% of the qualifications for a job[42] (because, remember, experience tells them they'll be rewarded based on performance, not potential), companies may default to trainings that support women to navigate these barriers rather than working to remove the barriers themselves.

It's also why Catalyst has seen time and again at our MARC workshops that well-meaning allies come to the realization that they have repeatedly encouraged their colleagues to "take a chance" on a woman when a man with the same qualifications would not have been talked about as being a calculated risk, but rather simply a good candidate. These allies now recognize they need to shift their framework from "Let's take a chance on her" to "Let's use the same objective criteria to evaluate this person as we have done for all candidates."

Not only is this approach more respectful and fair, it also has a better likelihood of setting women up for success. After all, if a woman is seen as someone the organization is "taking a chance on," any perceived missteps or failures can quickly become a self-fulfilling prophecy in the narrative that she wasn't ready for the job (also known as the "glass cliff"[43]). Instead, fairness dictates that the approach should be: "She is the best person for the job, and here's how we're going to support her." With this approach, she is set up to succeed, not fail.

I could go on and on about the motherhood penalty,[44] the second shift,[45] inadequate childcare,[46] the glass cliff,[47] gender bias in performance reviews,[48] and misogynoir (discrimination or prejudice toward Black women).[49] But my point is clear: Women are stalled, and that costs companies billions of dollars.

I want to add one final item for reflection: that one of our biggest obstacles to progress is, ironically, how much progress we've already made. When you take a cursory look at the workplace, you can see that women have come a long way since the days when all doctors were men and all nurses were women, and the employment ads were segregated by gender. But even after so much progress, women continue to slam up against barriers that men do not. Gender inequity has improved, for sure, but the problem has not been solved.

The truth is that we have come a long way, but we still have a long way to go. To make change, we all need to open our eyes—and our hearts.

Opening Eyes and Hearts

If you're exhausted reading these data points and experiences, I empathize. Now imagine living them!

At Catalyst, we use experiential, interactive learning to show, not tell, what it's like to be a woman in the workplace, particularly through our MARC program, which is designed to invite both women and men, at all levels, to cocreate an equitable workplace and community. I attended a MARC immersive program for leaders in Toronto in mid-2024 with nearly 40 senior leaders from several multinational organizations. We spent two days in a conference room exploring how gender stereotypes influence us all and what we can accomplish together as gender partners—assuming mutual accountability to close the gender gap for women at work and making change to benefit everyone, including men.

The facilitators, a man and woman, screened a Procter & Gamble (P&G) *Always* ad campaign called "Like a Girl."[50] Award-winning documentary filmmaker Lauren Greenfield asked teenagers and young people to imagine what it looks like to "run like a girl," "throw like a girl," or "fight like a girl," and the results were disturbing. The young people—both boys and girls—acted out the negative stereotype of a girl unable to proficiently accomplish any of these tasks, instead worrying about their hair, flapping their hands, and making no serious effort to throw an object for distance.

Why did these young people pantomime these actions? Because they had internalized insults about girls and physical activity. To them, what it means to run, throw, or fight "like a girl" was to be utterly ineffective and pathetic.

The commercial also demonstrated the ability to overturn stereotypes. Younger girls were shown forcefully kicking, running, and punching with confidence and power. The message was that gender-based insults are learned. That means they can be *unlearned*, even transformed into the language of empowerment. But it takes effort and intention to get there.

As the P&G *Always* ad campaign showed, the "like a girl" stereotypes run deep—even today, and even at young ages. The good news is that the incredible strides being made in women's sports and other areas are rapidly chipping away at these stereotypes. Similarly, the MARC facilitators showed another short film of children in the UK ages five to seven who were asked to draw pictures of a firefighter, surgeon, and a fighter pilot. The children assigned traditionally male physical characteristics and names to nearly all the pictures they drew. Then, a real-life firefighter, surgeon, and fighter pilot entered their classroom—all women—and the kids were visibly shocked.[51] To effectively nip stereotypes about women in the bud, we need to share with even the youngest children messages about equality.

Just as so many of us were conditioned to believe that girls and women can't run or throw and are unable to serve as firefighters, surgeons, and fighter pilots, many of us also are socialized to believe that women are not truly capable in workplace leadership roles. If they do succeed, there must be something wrong with them *as women* (they are more razor blade than cupcake).

Unfortunately, many of us grow up not only absorbing these messages but accepting them unconsciously,[52] failing to even notice when they play out in our adult lives, which also makes it harder to protest. The MARC facilitators screened one additional short film, part of an ad campaign by the mayor of London, showing weary commuters exiting an Underground station. The ad, titled *"Do you know what gender inequality at work looks like?,"*[53] shows a city employee at the bottom of the escalator and stairs; he tells the men to take the escalator and the women—even those who are older or who have baby carriages—to take the stairs.

Of course, it took the women longer to get to the top, and by the time they arrived, they were exhausted and irritated. And no one protested; everyone complied. When one woman with a baby stroller tries to take the escalator, the employee stops her and says, "It's just the way it is." Another woman helps her and the two of them carry the stroller up the stairs. If you've been to London, you know how deep some of the Underground stations are; there are *a lot* of stairs to get to the top.

When I participated in this training session, we women—spread across the room among the men—found each other's faces after the video ended. *Yep*, we said to one another wordlessly with our eyes. *That's what it's felt like for much of our careers*. When you consider the additional "rocks" women carry in our metaphorical backpacks (childcare, homecare, and eldercare being among the heaviest), it's hardly a surprise that this video resonates with so many.

The final activity in this section of the MARC immersive program was even more intense because it was so personal. The two facilitators took turns reading aloud examples of gender advantages and disadvantages. Our job was to listen, reflect, and consider if any of these statements sounded familiar:

> "When people think about leaders, they most often imagine people of your gender."
> "If you have children and continue to succeed in your job, people will not assume that you are a bad parent."
> "You are not expected to always be in a good mood or always smile."
> "You do not think about holding your keys in your hand when walking to your car or house."

And then we heard these examples:

> "Even if I spend as much time at home as my partner, I am less likely to manage an equal share of household responsibilities."
> "If I am hired or promoted, the decision was probably not impacted by whether I plan to have children soon."
> "I can get by in the workplace without putting extensive time or effort into my appearance."
> "If I move up in the organization, I don't feel much responsibility or expectation to help others of my gender progress."

If you are a woman, these statements may resonate with you personally; if you are a man, these statements may have you thinking about what the women in your life have experienced. At the MARC immersive program, men with daughters have said they found the statements especially powerful. Being a parent to a girl often is their starting place on the road to awareness and action of gender equity issues, and it is a welcome one. In MARC programming, we celebrate them starting there, but we also encourage them to move beyond it.

Alix has conducted many of these trainings over the past decade and has this to say:

I've heard women in their reflections in this exercise comment on how validating and assuring it was to hear their men colleagues reflect on their ahas, and yet how simultaneously disheartening it was to hear their colleagues—whom they had worked alongside for years and who have had mothers and wives and daughters this whole time—only just now coming to terms with these dynamics that women experience and accept as part of their daily lives. I've even heard a few women bravely say that as lovely as it is for these men to think about their daughters, it is also hard for them to hear because they don't want to have to be seen as someone's daughter (or wife, or sister) in order to be deserving of respect and dignity and fairness. While this has been a hard bit of feedback to be confronted with, most men have embraced the push.

A two-day program about creating a fair and equitable workplace may seem like overkill for leaders eager to get back to their workload. But Alix points out that the second day is where things really sink in for participants.

Almost always, across hundreds of sessions with thousands of participants around the world, there are men who say that they left the first day impacted yet also skeptical about how much of what was discussed is still true today and pervasive rather than one-off exceptions to the norm. They then inevitably go on to share that they brought it up over the dinner table with their wives and kids, that they called their daughter off at college, that they rang up a former woman colleague-turned-friend, and what they heard back was a resounding *ABSOLUTELY!*—and how struck they were by the conversations that ensued and how much of a mindset shift clicked into place for them as a result.

For me, one woman's terse statement summed up so well what it can feel like when you carry a heavier load just because you're a woman: "Hearing those statements was like a gut punch," she said.

Gender Diversity Is Good for Business Outcomes

In a boxing ring, a gut punch can wipe out your opponent and make you the winner. But in business, a gut punch affects not only the individual but others around them. The harm is not limited to the person receiving the punch. When a company is thriving, everyone who works there stands to benefit. When it's not, everyone stands to suffer.

The reality is that gender-diverse workplaces are *essential* for companies to thrive. In executive management, according to the International Labour Organization, the majority say that diversity improves their business outcomes (measured by profitability, productivity, talent attraction and retention, innovation and creativity, and positive reputation).[54]

Chevron CEO Mike Wirth shared with Catalyst the evolution of his thinking about gender balance at his company.[55] "In college, I always wanted to be on the project teams with some of the women students because they were the best students that would give you the best grade," he told us. "When I started at Chevron, my first three supervisors were women and they were still, to this day, three of the very best bosses that I've ever had, and relatively early on."

Later in his career, Wirth "was at a meeting with many of our senior women executives, and I was the only man in the room. After we went around for introductions and it was my opportunity to speak, my palms were sweaty, I had butterflies, and I realized what everybody in that room had felt many times being the only one."

He continued, "Our industry faces one of the biggest challenges mankind has ever faced. How do we go through an energy transition to get to a lower-carbon economy—to deal with the challenges of climate change? I need people from every country, every background, every racial and ethnic group, every way of thinking. And I need them to be able to bring their whole selves to work so we can solve these big challenges. I can't afford to *not* have a workforce that represents all of the people and all of the ideas, all of the creativity, all of the passion. It's really so core to our purpose."

Dow Chair and CEO Jim Fitterling echoes the idea that women bring diverse perspectives to teams. He told me, "They often just have a different approach to problems. Rather than getting into kind of a male-centric, stereotypical way of looking at things, they bring an alternate voice and a different way to look at it. It opens up people's thought process."

Our own data at Catalyst supports this finding that all employees and businesses benefit in myriad ways from diversity and inclusion:

- Talent retention: 20% of employees' desire to stay at their organization is linked to feelings of inclusion,[56] and 76% of employees say that organizations should take strides to ensure workplaces are diverse and inclusive of all employees.[57]

- Team performance and innovation: Overall experiences of inclusion predict 49% of team problem-solving and 18% of employee innovation.[58]

- Reputation and responsibility: Organizations with inclusive business cultures and practices are nearly 58% more likely to improve their reputations.[59]

- Financial performance: Many studies link diversity to indicators of profitability and financial health, including cash flow return on investment, gross and net margins, internal rate of return, investment performance, and market value.[60]

Likewise, McKinsey data demonstrates that "when companies are under extraordinary pressure to maintain financial performance while navigating a rapidly changing business landscape . . . diversity matters *even more.*" In the fourth edition of their "Diversity Matters" report series, published at the close of 2023 and drawing on data from 1,265 companies, 23 countries, and 6 global regions, McKinsey found that "companies with diverse leadership teams continue to be associated with higher financial returns. Our expanded dataset shows this is true across industries and regions, despite differing challenges, stakeholder expectations, and ambitions."[61] Not only is gender balance good for your company's financial health; employees want and expect it. In a Catalyst survey of 6,800 employees in 11 countries:[62]

- 93% say they want their organization to be vocal about its efforts to be diverse and inclusive; yet
- 24% see that their organization's senior leaders do not engage in these discussions.

Employees' desires are clear: Establishing a gender balance, as well as other forms of diversity, is important to them, and they want leadership to take an active stance and communicate clearly what is being done.

The bottom line: Progress for women is essential to maintaining a competitive edge and securing long-term success for your company.

Where Men Fit in This Equation

We have firmly established that women face tough challenges in the workplace. But men encounter obstacles, too, and many of them stem from the same systemic issues that affect their women colleagues. As we are about to explore in the next chapter, men must also cope with stereotypes that can inhibit them from expressing themselves authentically and achieving their full potential in the workplace.

Research finds that stereotypically masculine traits can become the default expectation for the behavior of all employees,[63] even though not all employees are rewarded for it to the same degree.[64] And it turns out that these traits don't align with how most men would authentically show up in the workplace; 75% of men say that they don't feel like their true selves when they're expected to be aggressive, independent, and competitive at work.[65] This, obviously, prevents men from displaying the full range of human behaviors that are available to them. It can also hamper their ability to advance in the workplace, form beneficial relationships,[66] and thrive in all the ways people, regardless of gender, want and expect to flourish at work.

We can do better—for men, for women, for everyone.

2

Why Workplaces Don't Work for Men Either

Men face challenges in the workplace, too, because of expectations and stereotypes for how men are "supposed" to act that seep into workplace cultures. They share powerful and resonant stories of being boxed in and shut down, experiences underscored by Catalyst data.

Women aren't the only ones stymied by norms and stereotypes. The expectations around how men "should" behave also start in childhood, and these masculinity norms get reinforced everywhere, including in the workplace.[1] What would it look like if we did away with "shoulds"? There are multiple ways to be a man, just as there are myriad ways to be a woman. Yet most boys grow up learning one fairly rigid path.

Gary Barker, CEO of Equimundo: Center for Masculinities and Social Justice, recalls being five years old and picking wildflowers for his mother. He told the crowd at a Catalyst event that he will never forget that an older child had laughed at him for this supposed "girly" behavior.[2]

Jane, a consultant who helps organizations build more inclusive cultures, spoke at the same event about how her professional and personal lives often overlap. While she encourages leaders to see men as individuals shaped by their unique backgrounds, cultures, and experiences (not just as a single group), she's also raising a Black son. As a mother, Jane is experiencing the impact of these rigid expectations firsthand. When her son was five years old, she received a call from his elementary school, saying he was being "too aggressive" during flag football at recess. Although most kids were using the phrase "take them down" as part of their play, Jane, the only parent of a student of color, was the only one contacted. That moment was a blow, showing her how rigid expectations around masculinity, combined with stereotypes, can affect boys differently. Far too often, Black boys must figure out how to be connected with their peers without being seen as threatening. As Jane puts it, her son can play a sport that requires physical aggression, but if he is Black, he can be aggressive *only up to a point*.

In his viral presentation for TED Women Talk, "A Call to Men," Tony Porter, CEO of the organization A Call to Men, shared that when he was 12 and living in New York City in the Bronx, he felt pressured by a troubled 16-year-old boy to engage in an act of sexual abuse against a neighborhood girl.[3] He admits that, at the time, he actually looked up to the boy, though now Porter recognizes that the boy was "up to a lot of no good." It was more important to him at age 12 to fit in "as a man" than to care about the girl. (Thankfully, he did not participate in the sexual abuse against the girl, but he did pretend he had done so to save face among his male peers.)

These stories about boys discovering that they must follow specific rules of behavior to fit in are heartbreaking and hard to hear. Yet too often, they are unexamined and undiscussed.

As a society, we may be working to raise our daughters more like our sons and encouraging them to be anything they want to be when they grow up, but do we have the courage and are we making the same effort to raise our sons more like our daughters? Are we focusing on their social and emotional development in the same way? Because for every young Hillary Rodham Clinton being told she could not become an astronaut, there is a young boy being told he cannot be a ballet dancer or a nurse or an elementary school teacher.

How has this happened? In the late twentieth century, and continuing through today, women's rights activists have justifiably called attention to inequities for women throughout society, including in the home and the workplace. Yet during this era, the constricting effects of gender expectations *for men* were not at the forefront of discussions about gender equity. As Andrew Grissom, director of community growth at Catalyst, has pointed out,

> By the 1970s and 1980s, women were making significant strides in the workforce, breaking new ground in the business world to the extent that the notion of women "having it all"—a successful career, family, and marriage—was a prominent cultural talking point. But something was missing.
>
> Nothing was changing at all for *men*. Men were still expected to be "providers," work long hours, and leave unpaid work, such as household chores and childcare, to women. Women were standing up for themselves, and men weren't invited to the conversation. In hindsight, it makes sense that some of them perceived gender equity as a zero-sum game that suddenly created a whole new group of competitors in the workplace and put them at a disadvantage.[4]

To achieve fairness for everyone in the workplace, we need to talk about the ways that men, like women, also suffer from narrow gender expectations.

Stereotypes About Gender Impact Men *and* Women

When I attended the Catalyst MARC program for leaders, I saw first-hand how stereotypes about gender permeate our everyday assumptions. Our two facilitators divided us into groups and instructed the women to write down all the words that came to mind when we remembered what we had been taught about femininity when we were growing up. The men were likewise told to identify the words that came to mind when they remembered what they had been taught about masculinity. We were allotted only a few minutes for this exercise, and my group had no trouble quickly calling out words and phrases that we recorded on the poster.

We then had the opportunity to walk around the room to see what the other groups had written on their posters. Perhaps not surprisingly, all four boards were nearly identical. For the "feminine traits" lists, the boards had variations of:

- Nurturing
- Submissive
- Caregiver
- Cheerleader
- Wife and mother
- Pretty
- Helpful
- Accommodating
- Soft-spoken

The "masculine traits" lists contained these words:

- Strong
- Provider
- Stoic
- No cooking or cleaning
- No crying
- Sexually active
- Athletic
- Angry
- Violent
- Protector

Next, we were told to write down the insults we were familiar with for people who did not conform to these traits as expected. Again, every group came up with nearly identical lists. (Content warning: This section contains hurtful words that reflect real gender stereotypes. We are including this content to demonstrate the ways in which they are normalized and reinforced.)

The insults for girls and women included:

- Tomboy
- Bitch
- Butch
- Slut
- Ugly
- Bad mother

And for boys and men:

- Sissy
- Girly
- Fag

- Crybaby
- Weak

It was sobering to realize that all of us in the room—men and women with vastly different identities and experiences—had come up with the same terms without consulting one another. All of us had been influenced by the dominant stereotypes about gender; had grown up learning similar and damaging messages about who and what we were expected to be; and had witnessed or even participated in driving others to stay in their "gender lane."

Clearly, we need to invite men and women to the conversation about the norms and expectations that everyone experiences and then reflect on how that may shape the ways we think and interact at work.

The Man Box

A useful way to think about masculine norms is through a concept known as the *man box*, which was developed by Paul Kivel of the Oakland Men's Project and advanced by Tony Porter of A Call to Men.[5] This concept refers to the socialization of boys and men in a way that directs them to conform to rigid, stereotypical behaviors and attitudes that box them in. Expectations include behaviors that many people believe are core to being a "real man," such as suppressing emotions, being self-sufficient, not forming deep friendships, acting tough, being heterosexual, having a strong sex drive, being aggressive, and being a provider rather than a caregiver.

Where do boys and men learn about these expectations of manliness? Everywhere—from their parents and family members, friends and classmates, coaches and teachers, social media influencers and celebrities, political and cultural leaders, and colleagues and managers.

Boys and men absorb these messages about manliness throughout their lifespan, so it's no wonder the ideas seep in and become internalized; they are inescapable.

We know that boys and men are exposed to these expectations—but does that mean they actually *conform* to them? After all, we're all exposed to messages every day that we reject. If we all did everything we were "supposed to," we would all exercise daily, eat well-balanced meals, and never make impulse purchases we later regret!

But it's different with messages about stereotypical masculinity. A survey of over 3,000 men ages 18 to 30 assessed the extent to which young men internalize the expectations of the man box. Brian Heilman, Gary Barker, and Alexander Harrison, authors of the 2017 research report *The Man Box: A Study on Being a Young Man in the US, UK, and Mexico*, confirmed that the man box "is alive and well. It has immediate, sometimes contradictory, and often harmful effects on young men and those around them."[6] Young men in the study confirmed they experience "overwhelming social pressure to fit into the man box." In other words, over time the man box becomes nearly impossible to escape.

The man box is a problem because it is harmful—to both the boys and men in the box as well as those outside it. Acting tough, repressing emotions, and failing to connect to other people comes at a steep cost with serious health care and societal implications. The authors of this man box report sound the alarm bell: "We must be worried about the mental health of young men. Their bravado and outward posture that 'all is fine' mask deep insecurities, depression, and frequent thoughts of suicide. These issues are all the more troubling because . . . those in the man box are even less likely to turn to peers and friends for help when they need it."[7]

An additional study confirmed this dismal finding. Researchers at UPMC Children's Hospital of Pittsburgh teamed up with Equimundo to create a standardized "man box" scale to measure the concept.[8] They found that men with high scores had higher rates of bullying behavior (including verbal, online, and physical) and sexual harassment. They also were twice as likely to experience depression or suicidal ideation.[9] "These findings highlight how detrimental harmful masculinities can be to the people who endorse them, as well as [to] their peers, families, and communities at large," said lead author Amber Hill.[10]

This research demonstrated that men who agree with the following five beliefs were much more likely to engage in violent behavior and experience poor mental health:

1. A man shouldn't have to do household chores.
2. Men should use violence to get respect if necessary.
3. A real man should have as many sexual partners as he can.
4. A man who talks a lot about his worries, fears, and problems shouldn't really get respect.
5. A gay guy is not a "real man."

Gary Barker summed up the situation. "When men embrace stereotypical ideas about manhood, they're also more likely to harm the well-being of others, as well as impact their own health in adverse ways," he said.[11]

The American Psychological Association (APA) agrees, noting that "men commit 90% of homicides in the United States and represent 77% of homicide victims. They're the demographic group most at risk of being victimized by violent crime. They are 3.5 times more likely than women to die by suicide, and their life expectancy is 4.9 years shorter than women's."[12] Moreover, boys are disproportionately diagnosed with attention-deficit hyperactivity disorder and disciplined at school. In short, says the APA, "traditional masculinity is psychologically harmful."[13]

The task now is to change these harmful attitudes to enable healthier versions of masculinity so that boys and men get the care they need. To this end, the APA in 2019 issued, for the first time ever, guidelines to help psychologists working with boys and men.[14] These guidelines range from encouraging positive father-child interactions in family relationships to supporting education that is responsive to boys' needs to finding ways to reduce boys' and men's levels of aggression and violence.

As Equimundo eloquently summed up the problem in their State of American Men 2023 report,

> Men in the US are in trouble. Many feel that their futures are uncertain and their identities are threatened . . . Many feel disconnected altogether and retreat to private lives of under-achievement, underemployment, online addiction, and to the pretense that they can go it alone. Some may find solace in misogyny and white supremacism . . . When two thirds of young men feel that "No one really knows me" . . . they reveal the fragility of their connections and relationships.[15]

Is This About "Toxic Masculinity"?

No, it's not. The term "toxic masculinity" is often used when people want to discuss men who are violent, aggressive, homophobic, and sexist. At Catalyst, though, we believe this term is counterproductive and often misinterpreted—and therefore we don't use it.[16]

For some, the term "toxic masculinity" suggests that there's something inherent about being a man that is toxic, and it places blame and shame on individual men. That is the opposite of what we believe. We agree with Richard V. Reeves, author of *Of Boys and Men* and founding president of the American Institute for Boys and Men. He writes, "Very few boys and men are likely to react well to the idea that there is something toxic inside them that needs to be exorcized. This is especially true given that most of them identify quite strongly with their masculinity."[17]

In the last few years this term has become more widely used, even in the workplace, and it is misleading and hurtful. Men are not toxic. Masculinity is not toxic. What *is* toxic is the way masculinity often is expressed culturally as a result of fixed expectations of what it means to be manly. For these reasons, we prefer the term "man box" because it's a clearer description of the ways in which boys and men may be trapped by something outside of themselves.

HAVE YOU HEARD THESE PHRASES?

Hint . . . They Reinforce the Man Box[18]

"Boys will be boys."

Bad behavior is not hardwired into boys' DNA. All people, regardless of gender, should be held accountable for their actions.

"That's not for boys."

The pressure to conform to gender stereotypes not only strengthens the man box but contributes to the gender pay gap and other gender divides. So-called "girly" colors, activities, and professions have equal value compared to their "manly" counterparts.

"Boys don't cry."

They do! We can all be sad sometimes, and we must let boys and men know that's okay. Try saying, "Help me understand what you are feeling right now," so boys and men can learn to identify, name, and own their feelings.

"It's just locker-room talk."

A lot of guys don't like to participate in sexist banter, or "locker-room talk," but they go along with it anyway. Knowing you're not alone in rejecting this practice can make changing the conversation easier. Almost any response is better than ignoring the situation. Commit to interrupting next time and saying something like, "Hey, let's leave locker-room talk out of this."

"Bros before hoes."

This language uses a vulgar term and should not be tolerated. Besides, building connections with women is just as important as doing so with other men. Don't let gender hold you back from forming meaningful relationships in life.

"I'm not gay, but . . ."

Because of harmful stereotypes suggesting that gay men are not "manly enough," physical touch and emotional vulnerability can feel like they're off-limits in friendships among men. But intimacy is an important element of all relationships.

"No one needs to hear my problems."

You'd be surprised by how many are willing to listen. Break the stigma around talking about mental health by making it okay to have courageous conversations. Say, "I'm always here for you if you want to discuss whatever is on your mind."

"Winning is all that matters."

Healthy competition can inspire you to learn, improve, and even innovate. But the process should be as important as the outcome. Don't get swept up in the drive to dominate.

"As the father of a daughter . . ."

Your daughter might be the reason you began to care about gender equity, but the cause is bigger than she is. Also, women should be regarded as individuals, not just as somebody's wife, daughter, sister, or mother.

It Starts in Childhood

Boys are socialized from young ages to fit into the man box. But they are not *born* inside this box. Judy Chu, a Stanford University lecturer and expert on boys' psychosocial development, has done research with four-year-old boys in prekindergarten who revealed themselves to be articulate and direct, even when discussing their vulnerabilities, and eager to connect openly and honestly with other boys. For example, as she shared with us at a Catalyst event, she observed two boys playing quietly with blocks in the corner. One boy noticed the other's sullen manner and said, "You don't seem to be very happy." The other replied, "I miss my mom." The first boy offered encouragement, saying, "That's okay. You always have your friends." The two then continued playing with blocks together.

Chu observed, "At four years old, these boys still felt free to talk about feelings in ways that older boys have learned can be unsafe. Evidence of boys' relational capabilities is consistent with what studies of infants have shown—that most people are born with a fundamental capacity and primary desire for close, mutual, responsive relationships."

However, as they grow and encounter societal pressures to conform to the man box, boys begin to adapt their behaviors in ways that can hinder their ability to connect with their peers. She also witnessed how boys learned to devalue and avoid behaviors they regarded as feminine. This was formalized through their creation of and participation on the "Mean Team," which reinforced a boys-versus-girls dynamic and hierarchy among the boys. One boy confided to Chu that "All of the girls in the class are my friends, but I act as though they aren't . . . because if Mike [the self-appointed boss of the "Mean Team"] finds out that I like the girls, he'll fire me from his club . . . That would be a real bummer, because then I won't be on a team."[19]

The boys wanted to connect to each other and have a sense of belonging—with girls and other boys—but to the extent that they felt compelled to prove their masculinity and show that they were one of the boys, they learned to behave as if these connections were unimportant. In short, they experience a crisis of connection that forces them to choose between expressing what they really think and feel (at the risk of being ridiculed or rejected) and conforming to social norms (at the risk of feeling that no one truly knows them).

In a Catalyst-hosted panel discussion about the way boys' relationships change as they learn the messages of the man box, Joseph Derrick Nelson, Swarthmore professor of Black Studies and Gender & Sexuality Studies, noted that schools in low-income communities of color in the US are shaped by the racism and poverty in which they exist. As a result, boys of color grow up in a racialized man box. Nelson explained that Black boys in particular grow up being told they are hyperaggressive, anti-intellectual, and hypersexual. "Teachers internalize these narratives, which are perpetuated through popular media," he said, and these narratives are then "mapped onto a broader crisis rhetoric that we hear in American society around Black boys and men . . . which then obscures teachers' ability to see Black boys' humanity and potential and promise." He added, "Even at the age of six, they already are deemed at risk or troublemakers."[20]

Chu wants teachers and parents to help create supportive spaces in which boys can safely show their vulnerable emotions, cry, and connect with other people. We all have a role to play in enabling boys, she said, "to develop the kinds of close, caring, emotionally responsive relationships that studies have shown are essential to their health and happiness."

Men sometimes cry, as all humans do. But they learn at a young age that crying is not "manly." Jason Wilson, author of *Cry Like a Man* and founder of the Detroit youth organization Cave of Adullam Transformational Academy (CATTA), shared in a presentation at a Catalyst event:

> Crying like a man is much deeper than shedding tears. It's about releasing the trauma and emotional pain we've been conditioned to suppress in our hearts and minds for years . . . During my era growing up, hip-hop was the music of our generation, and it was rare, if at all, you would see a young man smiling or expressing any other emotion outside of anger, seriousness, power, or strength. As a result, it transformed my loving smile, my kindhearted nature, into something less approachable. I became callous and held onto a lot of unresolved anger from my father not being in my life. I started suppressing the deeper emotions, and eventually that suppression led to depression . . . I slowly started drifting away mentally.

Wilson observes that his experience is common among boys and men, which has disastrous consequences: "Unfortunately, holding in negative emotions causes us to release them in unhealthy ways, such as spousal abuse, pornography, drug abuse, violence, and high-risk behaviors. This is why it's imperative that we learn how to cry like men, or cry like humans."[21]

What does the man box have to do with the workplace? Everything. When men are "boxed in," they are socialized to perpetuate a workplace culture that mirrors a number of stereotypically masculine traits, such as silence, toughness, and combativeness—which squelches the collaboration, innovation, and productivity of our teams. In addition, on an individual level, many men at work are suffering because of the toll the man box has on their mental health.

This Is What It Can Look Like When a Male Leader Is Open About His Emotions

Because men are not raised to reveal their emotions and connections to other people, it's all the more powerful when they buck convention and openly express emotions like affection, sadness, and gratitude in an emotional way. At work, the result can be transformative.

One of my favorite leaders and mentors is Alan Mulally. He grew up in a home that prioritized love and emotion, and he became one of the world's most successful CEOs, leading Boeing Commercial Aircraft through the 9/11 disaster and "saving" Ford Motor Company in his position as president and CEO during the Great Recession of 2008 through to 2014.

Alan communicates with empathy and a full spectrum of emotion, and he peppers his emails with hearts, smiley faces, and exclamation points, along with effusive language that includes the words "love" and "working together" many times over.

In February 2025, as the external environment changed quickly with the new administration, I reached out to Alan for some guidance on how to navigate my leadership internally and with select organizations who support us. He responded immediately:

From: Alan Mulally
Date: Tuesday, February 25, 2025
To: Jennifer McCollum
Cc: Sarah McArthur
Subject: Re: Working Together in this evolving environment

Hello Jennifer!

Really found your two emails very interesting and important!

Available now for one hour and then back at 6pm mt.

And available tomorrow after noon mt.

Love your leadership!

Thank you!

Alan

I jumped on the phone with him that day as he offered me his counsel and encouragement, and he followed up that evening:

From: Alan Mulally
Date: Tuesday, February 25, 2025
To: Jennifer McCollum
Cc: Sarah McArthur
Subject: Re: Working Together in this evolving environment

Great "Working Together" with you!!

Best thoughts are with your wonderful leadership!

Thank you!

Alan

I then realized I could use his guidance to help our Catalyst staff, Board, and the organizations we work with, so I expressed my gratitude and asked for his approval:

From: Jennifer McCollum
Date: Tuesday, February 25, 2025
To: Alan Mulally
Cc: Sarah McArthur
Subject: RE: Working Together in this evolving environment

Thank you, Alan.

I left with a renewed sense of how to evolve our Business Plan Review (BPR) and our Townhalls given your feedback, thank you. My biggest takeaway after hearing your perspectives on the external environment is this:

We need to watch and listen carefully to our Supporters in this extraordinary time and work together with ALL stakeholders to seek opportunities that may not be evident right now. This is the quote I'd like to use with my team, if it's okay to attribute it to you:

"We have entered the greatest unknown that I have ever seen in my lifetime, so remember: Change is a gem—you have to work together to figure it out!"

I told my Catalyst team all about you when I introduced your BPR and the Working Together (WT) leadership and management system, so I'd love to inspire them with your words, but only with your permission.

Jennifer

His final email to me confirmed I was on the right path:

From: Alan Mulally

Date: Tuesday, February 25, 2025

To: Jennifer McCollum

Cc: Sarah McArthur

Subject: Re: Working Together in this evolving environment

Hi!

So well said!

And including all stakeholders!

:)))

Very good!

Thank you!

Alan

On the surface, this email exchange may not look like much. But without exaggeration, when Alan sends along a personal note that leads with his emotions, I trust him even more. I look forward to every email and every conversation with him where he shares both his business perspectives and his feelings openly.

His display of emotion models for all of us what it looks like for men to be empathetic, vulnerable, and honest—all keys to the evolving expectations of leadership. The important element is not the emojis and exclamation points. It's the openness, generosity, and authenticity. For a man to be a great leader, he doesn't need to write emails like Alan. The lesson here is that embracing emotion can help build connections.

FLIP THE SCRIPT ON GENDER
STEREOTYPES ABOUT MEN

WHAT PEOPLE SAY: "He's so nice, but I just don't think he's got the stomach for leadership."

WHAT TO SAY INSTEAD: "Empathy is one of our values. He'd be a great role model as a leader."

WHY: Empathy is a leadership skill that men often do not receive "credit" for the way women leaders do—and men may even be penalized for it. But empathy is an essential skill that links to many positive outcomes, including increased experiences of inclusion, innovation, and productivity among teams.

TAKE ACTION: Assess leaders across a standard set of expected business practices rather than by gendered expectations of how men in leadership "should" behave. Ensure the espoused values of your organization align with the behaviors that are recognized and rewarded.

———————

WHAT PEOPLE SAY: "Suck it up and be a man."

WHAT TO SAY INSTEAD: "That sounds tough—what do you need most right now?"

WHY: Pressure to fit masculine norms, including those that demand displays of strength to mask vulnerability, can negatively affect mental health and relationship building. Men need latitude to express a full range of human emotions and behaviors rather than pressure to subscribe to certain traits such as toughness.

TAKE ACTION: When someone shares a problem with you, approach the situation with curiosity, show empathy, and provide support, not ridicule. Reframe vulnerability as an act of courage and strength, recognizing that it is a universal human experience, not a weakness.

WHAT PEOPLE SAY: "You can stay late, right? I figured your wife watches the kids."

WHAT TO SAY INSTEAD: "Before we determine project assignments, let's review everyone's upcoming schedules."

WHY: Stereotypical gender norms around caregiving and the division of responsibilities at home can inhibit progress toward equity. A third of working fathers aren't comfortable discussing childcare or family commitments with their employer.[22] Language like this undervalues men as fathers, pressures them to minimize perceived or actual family roles, and assumes women are default caregivers.

TAKE ACTION: Everyone has different commitments that can affect work schedules; don't assume availability based on perceived gender roles and responsibilities. Instead, be transparent about work-life priorities and encourage other men to do the same.

Addressing Men's Mental Health Is a Business Imperative

Nearly one in five men experience depression, according to the World Health Organization, but less than half will receive treatment.[23] In addition, the global suicide rate is over twice as high among men than women, according to the World Health Organization.[24] But because of stigma over mental health—for everyone and especially for men—too many people suffer alone.

And they carry their suffering with them everywhere they go, including to their workplace. Jeffrey Grange, president of Protector Plans, shared that men tend not to reveal these challenges to their employer because they fear that transparency will have a negative impact on their job security or that they will lose their status at work.[25]

Using data from over 7,000 men working in offices across 13 different countries, we found that when a workplace has narrow expectations about acceptable masculine behavior, masculine expectations in the workplace are high: 69% of men experience low psychological well-being compared to only 38% of men in organizations with low masculine expectations.[26] In addition, 34% of men experience high workplace withdrawal (e.g., neglecting tasks, being late for work, making excuses to get out of work) compared to only 5% of men in organizations with low masculine expectations.

Caring about employees' mental health is not only the right thing to do for workers, it's also the smart thing to do for the company. Costs associated with loss of productivity due to depression and anxiety are estimated at $1 trillion per year globally.[27] There is also evidence that depression and anxiety are associated with lost productivity because of absenteeism and presenteeism (when employees are present but unable to function completely because of illness or injury).[28] If an employee with diabetes or heart disease or cancer were not getting treatment, their manager might consider saying something helpful to motivate the employee to seek out health care. Businesses need to react to mental health challenges the same way they react to physical health challenges.

How Business Leaders Can Model New Examples of Masculinity

After hearing the stories of so many men who are struggling, and with the knowledge that many men in your workplace may be suffering silently and secretly, I strongly encourage executives and managers to take steps so men feel supported and psychologically safe at work. We know men need the help; our research shows that, for 3 out of 4 men, masculine stereotypes don't reflect the realities of their full selves, and nearly 9 in 10 men want permission to access traits outside the man box.[29]

One of the most important things you should do as a leader is *show you care.* Here are some different ways to express that message.

Be open. One way to encourage personal connection at work is by sharing information about your own life. Make yourself vulnerable and demonstrate that you, too, are a human being with the same frailties and challenges everyone else faces. Lead by example.

Invite different conversations. Create an environment in which men and women know they can talk about their personal lives and their inner lives—including the hard stuff like depression, anxiety, or other mental health challenges, grief and loss, divorce, physical health challenges, whatever it may be—without negative repercussions. They should know that sharing these things will be met with positive outcomes, such as support, empathy, community, and information about employee assistance programs. Your job as a leader is not to be a therapist, but the days of "leaving it at the door" are gone—or at least they should be if you want employees to thrive, stay, and perform. Prioritize well-being and belonging. Push for policy changes and inclusive, protective language. And remember that an open-door policy is nice in theory, but people won't take you up on it if you don't first earn their trust and take a more proactive approach to initiating and modeling different kinds of conversations. Which leads me to the next point . . .

Model meaningfully. Be the change you would like to see across your organization. This might mean demonstrating humility by publicly acknowledging a mistake and talking openly about how you are educating yourself to do better next time. It might mean being willing to get vulnerable and show emotions at work you might have previously considered off limits. It might mean choosing to tell stories about the sweet moment you had with your kid over the weekend rather than recounting the highlights of your golf game.

Jeffrey Grange recalls the first time he spoke at work about his own challenges with mental health. "I was in front of a room of 300 people. I was the most knee-knocking nervous I've been at any point in my professional career because I was in effect outing myself to my colleagues. What is remarkable is that every day since, it has been clear that my words really resonated because, as a leader, I made it okay to acknowledge that mental health is a serious issue."[30]

Extend these lessons into your home. Demonstrate that leadership extends beyond the workplace. Encourage men to use parental leave and when they do, congratulate them for embracing their caregiving role. Former P&G CEO David Taylor is proud that Pampers has ad campaigns featuring fathers changing their babies' diapers and that the Gillette razor brand has a product line specifically designed for caregivers to shave someone else. The ad campaign had a product line that featured a man shaving his older father's face.

Taylor shared at a Catalyst event: "We need to be intentional about showing men that they are equal partners in the family and doing unpaid care work like changing diapers, cleaning the floors, and doing the laundry—because this authentically represents the experiences of many men today. We use our advertising to reflect a world where we can all thrive—at home and in the workplace. But P&G is just one company."[31]

Think critically about what you reward, amplify, and measure. Modeling healthier and more expansive forms of masculinity is not an all or nothing that requires you to "throw out the old to embrace the new." In fact, some of the more traditional characteristics that we find within the man box—like strength, rationality, and decisiveness—and those outside of it—like vulnerability, empathy, active listening—are not mutually exclusive. Quite the opposite. You do not have to give up one to show the other. New models of masculinity do not require always leading with one way of being or another; it is about showing that you can bring all facets of who you are, in the moments that call for them, without feeling constrained to any one way of being all the time. Given this, the choices you make about what to lift up as examples of good leadership, the stories you recount, and the behaviors you reward both implicitly and explicitly send powerful messages that signal to others what is acceptable and what's not and shape the narrative around what "good" looks like.

Francesco Del Porto, president, region Italy, and global chief customer officer at the Barilla Group, adds,

> Breaking out of the "man box" truly resonates with me. Growing up in a traditional sales environment, I was surrounded by a culture where men were expected to lead in a certain way— tough, assertive, and rarely showing vulnerability. However, over time, I realized that this wasn't the kind of leader I aspired to be. Barilla implemented programs to challenge rigid notions of masculinity, such as workshops on emotional intelligence and leadership training that emphasize vulnerability and collaboration. I made a conscious effort to listen more, to open up to my team, and to create a space where empathy and authenticity are valued.
>
> When Barilla introduced the Barilla Global Parental Leave Policy in 2024, I personally championed it. I wanted my team to see that taking care of your family and being present isn't just accepted—it's respected. Today, I'm proud that my leadership team reflects a true balance of men and women, and that we foster a culture where everyone feels they can bring their full selves to work.

Is this work easy? Of course not. But it is critically important to creating healthier workplaces for everyone.

Men Are Not the Problem

In the previous chapter, we explored what holds women back, and we saw that stereotypical norms about gender play a huge role. But Catalyst finds that workplace cultures with narrow gender norms, including rigid expectations of what it means to be masculine, pose an obstacle for *everyone*, regardless of gender. Everyone suffers because they can't be themselves at work—which, as we've discussed, harms their ability to communicate, collaborate, innovate, and build the authentic relationships that lead to cultures of trust and engagement and strong organizational performance.

Men are not the problem when it comes to building gender-equitable workplaces. In fact, 97% of men want fair outcomes for employees at work, regardless of gender, and 59% of men intend to engage in gender partnership with coworkers through actions like discussing gender norms and exclusionary, biased, or otherwise harmful behavior.[32] Instead, it's masculine stereotypes that stall progress for individuals and their organizations alike.

There is no single "right" way to be a man, and social environments that encourage flexibility—rather than rigidity—allow everyone to thrive. Men, like women, should feel supported in embodying a full spectrum of human characteristics and behaviors, whether those characteristics and behaviors are stereotypically masculine, feminine, or otherwise. When they are able to do this, employees, leaders, and organizations can flourish.

3

The Personal Aspect: What Stops Men from Stepping Up for Women (and Each Other)

Many men want to be gender partners and close gender gaps in the workplace but face individual barriers like lack of awareness, knowledge of what to do or say, and concern over how others will react. These are all real obstacles, but the good news is they can be overcome.

Every time I speak on a stage about how to accelerate progress for women leaders, I start by asking the men in the audience to raise their hands. They usually are greatly outnumbered by the women, and they look around for each other, visibly uncomfortable. Then I say, "Thank you for being here; your full support is meaningful. Men across industries in the US make up more than 70% of senior leadership roles,[1] and we can't solve the problem of approaching gender balance across levels without you." Then I start a round of applause, honoring the men in the room.

Indeed, many men truly want to be advocates for women. At Catalyst, we focus on a set of progressively more engaged and impactful attitudes and behaviors that fall across what we call the "advocacy continuum."[2] Our MARC program enables participants to get from the first stage, being absent, to becoming an advocate:

THE ADVOCACY CONTINUUM

ABSENT
Unaware of issues of gender inequity.

AWARE
Aware of issues, but not fully aware of the impact.

ACCEPTING
Recognizes that issues are real barriers, but not yet engaged in making change.

ACTIVE
Engages when asked.

ADVOCATE
Proactively seeks opportunities to enhance gender inclusion.

1. **ABSENT:** Not plugged in to the topic and, as a result, unaware that when it comes to fairness across gender, gaps (still) exist.
2. **AWARE:** Knows that there are issues and aware of what those issues may be, but not fully on board with their role in addressing them or why it matters.
3. **ACCEPTING:** Acknowledges and understands that there are barriers that cause real impact, but not yet personally invested or involved in making change.

4. **ACTIVE:** Gets involved and takes action when others ask, in response to expressed needs.

5. **ADVOCATE:** Is proactive about taking action; identifies needs without being asked and seeks opportunities to reduce barriers and enhance inclusion.

We believe moving along this continuum can create real change, and we also know from Catalyst research that it can be challenging for some—men in particular—to take the first step.

A whopping 86% of men told us that they want to call out sexism in the workplace, but only 31% feel confident enough to do it.[3] Other research has shown that there is a serious cost to being a bystander and not speaking up when witnessing discriminatory behavior. According to a fascinating 2024 study, "People Who Accommodate Others' Sexist Views Are Themselves Perceived to Be Sexist," men can face negative career consequences when they fail to speak up in the face of a colleague's sexist comment, even if they themselves are not engaging in sexist behavior. These bystanders are assumed to be sexist too. Meanwhile, the study found, men who challenge other men's sexist comments are viewed more favorably by their colleagues, both men and women.[4]

We wanted to understand why so many men don't step up for women, and for each other, since the overwhelming majority desire to do so. What is stopping them?

I wish I could tell you that there is just one stumbling block—and if we removed it, all would be well. But nothing is that easy! In fact, men are hampered by a combination of personal and organizational factors. We challenged our research team to identify the main factors so we could better enable leaders to overcome them.

Three personal factors can get in the way of men progressing along this spectrum:[5]

- **FEAR**—"*This is going to be a problem for me*": Concern that advocating for women will be at their own expense
- **IGNORANCE**—"*I don't see the problem*": Lack of awareness or clarity about sexism
- **APATHY**—"*It's not my problem*": Lack of personal interest or agency to make change

Identifying these roadblocks is crucial so that we can better show men how they, and everyone, benefit through gender partnership.

FEAR: "This Is Going to Be a Problem for *Me*"

Some men worry that advocating for women will result in a loss or penalty for men. In other words, if women win, men lose. We call this "zero-sum thinking," or the "But what about me?" response. It is the result of anxiety that one's status, resources, or job will be taken away and given to someone else. The more people believe that men suffer job losses on account of efforts to increase gender diversity, the less likely they are to express an interest in participating in advocacy efforts.[6]

But success and fairness for women is not at the expense of men. To the contrary, men benefit from a more gender-balanced and inclusive workplace, which enables them to break free of the unhealthy man box.[7] Inclusive work cultures promote healthy rather than combative relationships, with higher levels of trust and stronger team dynamics.[8]

Additionally, as we already discussed in chapter 1, research consistently shows that diverse teams outperform those that lack diversity.[9] Inclusion of diverse perspectives drives creativity, problem-solving, and employee engagement.[10] When teams include gender diversity, everyone benefits.

A similar concern is that it's not fair to men to advocate for women because everyone should have to work equally hard to earn equal rewards. This way of thinking stems from a misunderstanding over meritocracy, or the "But what about merit?" response—the concern that women who advance at work may not necessarily deserve to progress and that when they do so, they are subverting the noble goal of meritocracy. Belief in meritocracy is belief in the idea that merit, or talent, is the best way to assess who is best suited for different positions and to determine who should be rewarded.

The problem is that meritocracy does not truly exist—or, where it does, not everyone has fair and equal access to it.[11] Individuals experience both visible and invisible disadvantages and advantages that can, respectively, subvert or benefit their work performance. While some people face challenges such as lacking access to reliable or affordable child- or elder care, others may be advantaged from, for example, having a spouse who stays at home (enabling longer work hours and fewer work-life constraints) or having access to professional networks through family connections, giving them a leg up over their colleagues. In other words, two people may work equally hard and in equally competent ways, displaying equal merit, but the one who has advantages is better positioned to come out ahead.

Catalyst conducted research to see what happens when women and men use identical career advancement strategies. Did doing the same things yield the same career outcomes? No. In fact, we found that when women did all the things they have been told will help them get ahead—using the same tactics as men—they still progressed less than their male counterparts and experienced slower pay growth.

Our study followed 3,345 "high potentials" who stayed on a traditional career path after graduating from a full-time MBA program. We explored the impact of their career advancement strategies—such as pushing to be involved in high-profile projects, ensuring their manager was aware of their accomplishments, communicating their willingness to work long hours and on weekends, and proactively developing new skills through courses and workshops—with respect to their career advancement, compensation growth, and satisfaction with career progress.[12]

We discovered that similar approaches to career management resulted in different outcomes for women and men:

- Doing "all the right things" helped men, but not women, advance further and faster.
- Men advanced further than women, regardless of which approaches they took to achieve career growth.
- Men's compensation grew faster than women's, regardless of strategies used.

Our research finds that, despite the myth of meritocracy providing an equal playing field, meritocracy is not, in fact, equitable. Indeed, in "The Paradox of Meritocracy in Organizations," researchers demonstrated that when an organizational culture promotes meritocracy, the outcome ironically is that managers tend to show bias in favor of men over equally performing women.[13] Meritocracy may be a worthy aspiration, but it is not naturally occurring—it requires intention and a commitment to promoting inclusion and removing barriers if it is really going to be accessible to all and enable organizations to achieve the goals a meritocracy is intended to achieve.

Another type of fear is negative repercussions from other men, stemming from the concern about losing social and political capital among their male peers if they are seen as defying norms. They don't want to be the guy who makes other guys look bad. They don't want to be the guy who other guys feel like they can't talk openly around. They don't want to be the guy who disrupts the status quo. Our data shows that most men want gender equity,[14] so this fear may not be as warranted as they may perceive, but it is an extremely powerful driver of behavior (or lack of action in this case) nonetheless.

Finally, the fear I've noticed more than any other is the fear of making a mistake by saying or doing the wrong thing. A senior director in financial services said it to us best: "You know that you should say something, but there's that little voice in your head that tells you not to rock the boat. It comes from fear. Whether it's fear of embarrassment, fear of ostracization, fear of conflict, or fear of not having the right words."[15]

I remember when my husband, Chip McCollum, told me that a highly qualified woman a few levels below him was up for a promotion but there were whispers that she lacked confidence. When I asked if there was anything he could do to support her, he said, "I'm not sure what I can do, given I'm not her manager, and it could be perceived as unwelcome intervention." We discussed the role that he might play in using his influence and seniority to publicly recognize her excellence— or take her to lunch and offer his observations, experience, and counsel. It took a little push and encouragement, but it was enough for him to overcome his fear and act. She was promoted soon thereafter.

I totally understand the fear of saying the wrong thing; we all face that sometimes! But before the fear stops you, remember that if you speak up with good intentions and humility, people will forgive you if you use a word that's outdated, or if you express yourself clumsily. We're all human, and we've all been there. If we allow our fear to stop us, change will never happen.

IGNORANCE: "I Don't See the Problem"

Another reason some men may choose not to step up for women is that they are uncertain about what to do because they're not clear about the obstacles that women face. This is nothing to be embarrassed about; as we've seen, the barriers are multilayered, complex, and sometimes even invisible. No wonder so many people—women and men alike—may have difficulty seeing the problem!

"We all have blind spots," Balkrishan "BK" Kalra, president and CEO of Genpact and Catalyst board member, told me. "I learn by making it a practice to be curious and challenge my thinking and then encourage everyone across our company to do the same."

Why do we have trouble seeing the obstacles? And what is sexism, anyway?

WHAT IS SEXISM?

Sexism is such a loaded, divisive word and can mean different things to different people. So I asked Alix Pollack, one of our thought leaders at Catalyst, to break it down. Here is what she says:

> If you look sexism up in the dictionary you will find something along the lines of "unfair treatment or prejudice based on a person's sex or gender." Clear enough, and surely most people could rattle off a definition like that (or easily find one). But defining it and understanding it can be two very different things. What makes sexism *sexism*, as opposed to your run-of-the-mill unkindness or unfairness, for example? And is sexism really that easy to spot in our day-to-day lives and in our workplaces?
>
> Assumptions, misconceptions, and stereotypes about gender and sexual orientation are common and inevitable. When those ways of thinking are used to rationalize discrimination, mistreatment, or objectification, *that* is sexism.[16]
>
> Sometimes, sexism is overt. It's unmistakable—intentional, visible, unambiguous. Think *Mad Men*, the

television show about a 1960s advertising agency run by men, with women relegated to clerical and secretarial positions even though many of them were more competent than the men in charge, and where demeaning or inappropriate comments directed at women were pervasive and normalized.[17] Overt sexism, expressed in negative attitudes and behaviors toward a person based on their sex (like the belief that women are incompetent), is also referred to as hostile sexism and is what most people think of when they think of sexism.[18] We all know it when we see it, and it is not, unfortunately, a thing of the past.

The fact that it is less common these days, however, together with the reality that it's what most people associate with the idea of sexism, leads to ignorance about issues of sexism because many people see sexism as no longer being a problem. But there's more to the problem than hostile sexism and overtly sexist behaviors. There are other forms of sexism you may know less about: covert and benevolent sexism.

Covert sexism is subtle, hidden, or invisible, because it is built into social and cultural norms.[19] This form of sexism is still common, but it can fly more under the radar. It's the stuff that might leave you feeling just a little bit uncomfortable, but if you tried to retell the story of what happened, people might dismiss it as being in your head. It's the stuff that leaves you questioning, "Wait . . . was that sexist?" (Hint: If you have to ask, the answer is likely yes.) It's the "just a joke," "didn't mean anything by it," "only trying to help" comments and behaviors that can seem innocuous in isolation but add up to death by a thousand cuts. It's the stuff easily invisible to those not looking for it, but painfully evident to those systematically on the receiving end of it.

Benevolent sexism comes from a well-meaning place (e.g., the belief that women are more compassionate) that is nonetheless rooted in stereotypical attitudes based on someone's sex.[20] It's the compliments that don't really feel like compliments, the comments meant to offer praise that actually feel belittling, the knight-in-shining-armor behavior toward a woman who actually just wanted to make a decision or take an action for herself. Again, subtle, easy to miss, and not the stuff of sexist tropes . . . but nevertheless behavior that can perpetuate unhelpful dynamics and deepen gender divides rather than closing gaps.[21]

When men do see sexism and choose to respond, we have found that up to 74% of men reported saying they would respond to instances of sexism *in a benevolently sexist way*—that is, unintentionally meeting sexism with, well, more sexism.[22] Benevolent sexism refers to comments or actions toward women that are masked in chivalry, protection, and affection but that in reality serve to reinforce women's traditional roles in society and keep them subordinate.[23] So, while these men have good intentions—to interrupt a sexist comment at work—they are unintentionally maintaining the status quo, ignorant that they themselves are contributing to this dynamic.

It's easy to mistake benevolent sexism as flattery because of the seemingly positive nature of the stereotypes. For example, someone might state that men and women should hold different roles in the home and at work because they have different characteristics and capabilities.[24] In this scenario, they might justify the underrepresentation of women in positions of power by saying that women are naturally more gentle than men and lack masculine qualities, such as competitiveness or aspiration for power and dominance, that are necessary for business success. But it's a mistake to think that women are necessarily more gentle or less competitive than men. Rather, these traits are shaped by societal expectations and roles over the course of our lives.[25]

As McKinsey senior partners Kweilin Ellingrud, Lareina Yee, and María del Mar Martínez explain, if a woman's résumé suggests active parenting (such as a mention of being a member of the PTA), she is about 87% less likely to be called into an interview and get the job.[26] Even if we hold mothers in high esteem, we may also hold a bias against them by assuming they will prioritize their children instead of being an exemplary employee. We need to watch out for this form of sexism too.[27]

Here's a beautiful example of a male boss overcoming benevolent sexism. When Amy Wilson, general counsel and corporate secretary for Dow, was on her second parental leave—home with a newborn and a two-year-old—her boss called with an offer. Would she consider relocating to London for an exciting six-month assignment?

Amy was intrigued. She and her husband got out a whiteboard and wrote out all the pros and cons of every scenario. A few days later, she called her boss and told him that it was too short of an assignment for her and her husband to make it work with all the trade-offs that would be required. She added that if the offer had been for a longer move, that would be different.

"And he was great," Amy told me. "He said, 'I totally understand, and you're proving to me that you have good judgment. This won't count against you.' And then he said the best part: 'People told me that because you're on maternity leave, I shouldn't even offer you this opportunity. But I didn't want to make this decision for you.' That was a wow moment for me—that he didn't presume my decision even though

I was a young parent. And that he also wouldn't have presumed if I'd had aging parents, or some other set of considerations."

A boss with noble intentions—thinking he or she is trying to help out a team member who's on parental leave—might not even mention the opportunity. But a gender partner who understands the importance of fairness and equal opportunities, like Amy's boss, makes the offer.

Now Amy pays it forward by doing the same thing. "I've been in leadership team discussions where I've said, 'Time out, everybody. We should not make that decision for this person. We need to let them make the decision.' In a lot of cases, it's important for them to simply know that they were being considered. Otherwise, they just see someone else get the job. That's what happens when you make the decision for them."

In fact, two weeks later, Amy's boss called back and said, "You said that six months was too short. But would you consider a three-to-five-year assignment in Switzerland?" For that decision, Amy didn't need the whiteboard. She said yes right away. She and her husband moved to Switzerland, and her husband sold his law practice and became a stay-at-home dad for three years.

See what happens when you remove benevolent sexism? Amy was given the opportunity to fulfill her potential, and her husband found fulfillment by serving in a caretaker role.

FLIP THE SCRIPT ON BENEVOLENT SEXISM[28]

WHAT PEOPLE SAY: "Go easy on her—we shouldn't talk about women like that."

WHY IT'S SEXIST: While it can be natural for some to feel that they should be protective of others, the idea that men should protect women assumes that women are weak and dependent on men.

This assumption is damaging to women and often leads them to be assigned less challenging tasks in the workplace, effectively stunting their potential for growth and success. It can also prevent them from getting critical feedback necessary for their growth and development.[29]

WHAT TO SAY INSTEAD: "I get what you're saying, but that's feedback you should give her directly. And you might consider what it's like for her to be a woman at this company and how that likely impacts her leadership opportunities and the support she may need. I'll speak for myself and say that's something I'm working on."

TAKE ACTION: Shift your approach from protection to support. Everyone needs organizational support to thrive.

WHAT PEOPLE SAY: "Women are better bosses than men. They're more caring and nurturing."

WHY IT'S SEXIST: While being caring and nurturing are important human traits, it's not fair to assume that women always have those traits (and, relatedly, that men don't). This stereotype also leads women to be assigned more menial, administrative tasks that are not part of their job description.[30]

WHAT TO SAY INSTEAD: "I can think of plenty of women who are great managers. I'd like to see more leaders across the board demonstrate the skills I've seen from those women."

TAKE ACTION: Avoid generalizing and stereotyping, even in positive ways. If you are thinking of caring and nurturing women as counterexamples, be specific about what makes those women good managers and connect that to characteristics of good leadership, not gender stereotypes.

WHAT PEOPLE SAY: "How would you feel if someone made a comment like that about your wife or daughter?"

WHY IT'S SEXIST: While the intention is to shift the target to elicit empathy, this type of remark makes it seem as though women should be treated equally only because they are similar to people who men care about at a personal level, and not simply because they are fellow humans.

WHAT TO SAY INSTEAD: "I don't agree with that. It's not what I'd want for my wife or daughter, but it's also not what I want for anyone I work with."

TAKE ACTION: Avoid centering your comments around the notion that women are only worth defending or supporting because we know and love women in our lives. You can reference women you know to support a broader point; just don't make them the only point.

APATHY: "It's Not My Problem"

A third factor that leads many men to remain silent is apathy. Often, having a lack of concern stems from the belief that the problems women face don't affect men too. In fact, workplaces that don't work for women also don't work for men, and when women suffer, there's a ripple effect that everyone experiences. Because of apathy, some men see problematic behavior at work but let it slide.

At Catalyst, through our research collection and MARC trainings, we regularly hear stories from men across levels who theoretically want things to change but grapple with apathy they have experienced and witnessed in their colleagues. Often, men make themselves vulnerable and confide things in us that they haven't told anyone else. They reflect on how they might have supported fairness and inclusion conceptually but never felt like the issue of gender really had anything to do with them and their jobs. They say things like, "I knew my company was focusing on gender equity but I didn't feel strongly about it one way or another. It was just something happening out there that didn't impact me or my day-to-day . . . or so I thought."

Conversations with women colleagues, family members, or training experiences like MARC are often the impetus for a spark to get from apathy to commitment—especially when those "aha" moments are met with empathy and an opportunity for dialogue. But that, unfortunately, doesn't always happen. In one comment that stayed with me, a mid-level director in education—who did not feel free to share his perspective when it differed from his manager's—told us, "You need an organization that is open to challenge, is open to dissent, is not a 'yes sir, yes ma'am' type [of] organization. You have to value disagreement. You need an underlying culture that values critique and values conflict."

One executive I spoke with, Hal (not his real name), observed that in large corporations with thousands of employees, organization-wide policies often are an essential tool. But companies need to be careful about the ways that employees may react. "I want diversity, but it has to occur in partnership with all the stakeholders, not just top down," he said. Instead of making men feel like they are being forced and threatened by mandates, Hal advises leaders to first use positive energy to encourage a shift toward gender equity. "I explain a vision for what we want to create. And as a leader, I model these behaviors. If you leverage certain natural dynamics that you find in the team, I think it probably closes fewer doors." This kind of approach is so important in encouraging and supporting men as they step out of apathy into action.

What Does Action Look Like?

When someone overcomes their fear, ignorance, and apathy, they are ready to act. But taking that first step is not easy for everyone. For example, let's say that three men and one woman are in a meeting to discuss internal applicants for a newly developed role that is critical to managing efficiency in remote team operations. When reviewing a woman's qualifications, the male team leader says, "I thought she came across as a little aggressive." The room goes quiet for a split second; the woman looks down at her phone; and the conversation continues.

With the leader in the room, it wouldn't be surprising if you chose to say nothing. In fact, when our research team asked men what they would have done, a mid-level manager in the energy sector told us, "My last company was a construction company, and there was a lot of talk objectifying women. A lot of that came from senior leadership, and [it] created this . . . locker room culture. And so, I would say at that company, I was far less comfortable sticking my neck out."[31]

His response was not atypical. In fact, our research conducted in the United States, United Kingdom, Canada, and other countries uncovered four categories of actions men can take when they encounter sexism conducted by other people:[32]

- **Directly interrupt:** Comment on the inappropriateness of a sexist comment, either in the immediate situation or after it has occurred; attempt to educate the colleague who made the comment; or report the offense.

  Example: "A colleague was talking about women not being able to do something and saying they should be in the kitchen. I said that is not acceptable to say that, and you should know better."—an entry-level/non-management employee in resources, utilities, and energy working in Australia

- **Redirect:** Attempt to sidestep the sexist behavior and keep the conversation focused on the current task or redirect the conversation.

  Example: "A number of men were commenting on the appearance of women (in their absence) over drinks . . . I didn't say anything and tried to bring up different angles/topics to steer the conversation away. But I never said that it wasn't right to talk in that way."—a first-level manager in resources, utilities, and energy working in Ireland

- **Unassertively react:** Show disagreement through nonverbal cues like eye-rolling, passive-aggressive comments, or humor or sarcasm.

  Example: "Derogatory comments were made about an individual who was not present. I expressed my disapproval by jokingly saying . . . 'You're going to get us fired.' I didn't want to cause hard feelings with the person involved, but still wanted to express that I didn't want to continue that conversation."—a second-level manager in manufacturing working in the United States

- **Do nothing:** Ignore the situation and/or rely on others to address it.

  Example: "My boss at the time made an insensitive comment about a newly hired woman leader. I was a new employee and did not feel comfortable telling my boss that I thought that his comments were not appropriate."—a first-level manager in manufacturing working in the United States

We asked men how likely they were to engage in each of these behaviors in response to a colleague's sexist remark.[33] Less than half of respondents felt comfortable directly interrupting. Nearly two-thirds of men indicated they would redirect, almost a quarter said they would react unassertively, and 20% said they would do nothing.[34]

Men's responses to sexist events

The likelihood of engaging in different types of interrupting behavior:*

46%	**65%**	**24%**	**20%**
Directly interrupt	Redirect	Unasserrtively react	Do nothing

* Numbers exceed 100% because men could choose multiple responses.

"It's very rewarding when you have a conversation with someone [about advocating for women] and they say, 'Okay, well, I get it, I'm going to try to change that,'" a senior director in energy told us. "The motivation [is] opening people's eyes that we're really better if we have a workplace that works for everybody."[35]

Darryl White, CEO of Bank of Montreal (BMO), adds that when you're consistent and persistent in showing how important it is to make workplaces work for women, the efforts pay off. "BMO has cultivated that culture for a long time," he told me, "even before we had that language. In fact, since the 1990s, when we began to publish white papers on the topic, we have consistently led with this at the heart of our management ethos and culture, though we still have work to do."

Engaging Men to Step Up

Now that we have identified the personal factors that prevent some men from stepping up, we are ready to overturn them. And nothing stops sexist behavior quite like a leader taking aggressive action against it. Christian, an executive at a global pharmaceutical company in Europe, described his "zero tolerance" policy.

He recalled, "A few weeks before I took over a position at a previous company, there was an incident where a male coworker poured paper waste over the head of a female coworker. The incident was investigated and my predecessor reprimanded the male coworker. On the first day of my job, I asked the man into my office and said, 'This situation came to my attention. I wasn't in charge when it happened. But I can tell you this: If something like this happens under my watch, you are out on the same day.'"

While this incident was an extreme example of overt harassment, women often experience sexism and discrimination in the workplace in much more subtle ways—and Christian acknowledges that these instances can be difficult to recognize and address.

He refers to the "gray zones" in which women can find themselves, "where the person being accused can make a convincing argument for their actions and be given the benefit of the doubt." Meanwhile, the woman on the receiving end of this behavior may, if the incidents are downplayed by the perpetrator and those in charge, start to question herself: *Is this genuinely sexism, or am I reading too much into what's happening?*

"This type of situation causes self-doubt in victims, and that's what makes being in the gray zone so toxic," Christian said.

He points out that many women get stuck in the gray zone "because there's always a fear of retaliation, and in many cases, the victim doesn't want to have the spotlight shone on them. From a leadership perspective, the subtle sexism that happens in the gray zone isn't so clear that you can directly address it."

Christian said that getting to the bottom of subtle sexism "involves difficult, awkward conversations—and you will find more and less courageous people." At the end of the day, though, doing so is a leader's responsibility. "Once the line is crossed, there should be zero tolerance."

When a sexist remark or act takes place at work, adds Darryl White, it's important to "stand in front of it immediately and visibly in front of other people and stop the behavior. I've watched other leaders and learned from them as they do this effectively, and so then I've done it myself." As with Christian, Darryl differentiates between overt and covert acts that diminish women. "When the behaviors are less overt, having private, one-on-one conversations with the colleague has often revealed a lot. Sometimes the colleague just doesn't realize the extent of their impact on others." He recalls a specific incident with a colleague who had a pattern of being condescending and "almost bullying" with other colleagues, men and women alike. "When I confronted this colleague, I found it interesting that he was surprised his behavior was noticed. He made a commitment to change it."

Did the colleague stick to their commitment? Yes, he did, Darryl reports. Had Darryl not intervened, the bad behavior would have continued. When a strong leader models gender partnership by calling out problematic behavior, employees can transcend fear, ignorance, and apathy.

4

The Organizational Aspect: How Companies Perpetuate a Climate of Silence

If you've ever worked at a company where employees are fearful of speaking up about unsafe or unfair conditions, you're familiar with a workplace culture that we at Catalyst call a "climate of silence." Leaders can shape an alternative culture that fosters gender partnership and all the benefits that come with it.

We've just uncovered that many men want to do the right thing but might not act because of personal factors that inhibit them from speaking up or taking action. Our research further identifies an organizational inhibitor, a *climate of silence*,[1] that also prioritizes the values of the man box. In a climate of silence, men and women both lose: All employees feel as though they can't constructively speak up about work-related problems, concerns, or challenges; men and women who want to speak up when they experience or witness discrimination and bias fear that doing so puts their career at risk; and anyone being discriminated against is left without someone to advocate for them.

How a Climate of Silence Perpetuates Inaction—and What Men Can Do About It

Catalyst research finds that 44% of men say there is a climate of silence in their workplaces,[2] meaning they work in an environment where employees believe that speaking up will bring negative repercussions or that their voice won't be heard. It's therefore no surprise that, in a climate of silence, men report a greater likelihood of doing nothing to interrupt sexism: 39% of men working in organizations with high levels of silence report doing nothing, compared to 5% of men in organizations with lower levels of silence.[3]

It's not that employees always make a calculated decision to be silent in the face of sexism. Rather, what happens is that employees unexpectedly find themselves in a high-pressure situation and may simply "freeze."[4] Or, they may decide not to respond in the moment and instead take some time to consider what to do. Keeping quiet is a behavior that employees learn over time as a response to their organizational climate.[5]

In our study of men across job levels working in three multinational corporations, we found that whether or not a man worked within a climate of silence impacted his response to a colleague making a sexist comment. As the climate of silence became stronger, they were 30% less likely to question their colleague and 35% less likely to comment on the inappropriateness of their colleague's comment.[6]

As an interesting aside, we found that when there's a climate of silence, men are significantly more likely to choose indirect styles of confrontation and respond to sexism with sarcasm or humor. This is noteworthy because it shows that when organizational silence prevails, men don't feel that they have as wide a range of options available to interrupt sexist behavior. It's also notable that sarcasm and humor inhibit getting directly involved.

The good news is that if much of this behavior has been learned, it can also be unlearned. The norms and behaviors that support a climate of silence can change, and one of the best and most effective places for this change to start is at the leadership level. As a leader, you have the unique privilege to inspire this change because when employees see that authority figures can speak up and action results, they feel invited to do the same. Senior managers are particularly influential in either reinforcing silence or inviting employees to speak up and be heard.[7]

When Joseph began his job at a manufacturing company, he was immediately faced with a problematic circumstance. "I had a number of female workers complain unanimously about the behavior of one male leader," he says. Joseph took charge of the situation. In an independent investigation, the allegations were corroborated. He took ownership and did the right thing for his team. "When it comes to sexism and harassment, I have zero tolerance," he says. "There's no room for that kind of behavior. When it occurs, we are past the point of coaching, supporting, or helping people understand. The leader was let go."

By being proactive, Joseph demonstrates how men can be strong gender partners and help spark broader culture change. Ideally, though, male leaders will have support from their organizations. Joseph believes that organizations must "train and sensitize leaders" so they can recognize and respond to sexism.

There are, of course, many examples of sexist behavior that are far less overt and unlikely to be fireable offenses. Calling out egregious instances of sexism can be powerful and needed but a "call in" culture where missteps are treated as learning opportunities rather than moments to shame and blame is equally essential for driving positive change. In these moments, gender partners can "call in" colleagues by leading with curiosity and assuming positive intent. This might sound like, "Help me understand what you mean by that?" or "What I heard was X, but I am not sure that's what you meant. Can you clarify?" It also entails choosing moments and methods of naming and redirecting the behavior, like pulling them aside after the fact for a private conversation that might sound like, "Hey, I'm not sure if you realized but when you said A it made me and I suspect others feel B and I wanted to let you know." These "calling in" approaches are invitational rather than accusatory and therefore allow the person to process and find ways to do better going forward based on a desire to grow, not just to comply.

There are many ways leaders can defuse sexist behaviors. For example, if men alone are asked for data insights or P&L analyses, or to confront a challenging client situation, and women alone are tasked with delivering sensitive news that might upset staff, a leader could announce that, going forward, these responsibilities will be rotated so that everyone shares in these tasks. Or, if someone says that a particular woman is great at her job but not a friendly person, a leader could comment that they never hear men described in the same way.

Leading by example is key to opening the door to communication. Leaders should model gender partnership not only by abstaining from sexist behaviors but also by calling out sexism to show that the act of calling out is expected of everyone.[8] "It takes courage to shift a culture," a senior director in financial services told us. "If you don't have a culture that invites courage to challenge the status quo to speak up, then you normalize certain behaviors."[9]

Our data shows that the more men perceive that their workplace has a climate of silence, the higher the likelihood that they will suppress their desire to speak up and the higher the likelihood they will associate certain potential costs with speaking up, including being viewed as a complainer, a troublemaker, or an annoyance. They may also be hesitant because speaking out might damage their relationships with supervisors or threaten their career security.[10] I encourage you to do the right thing, even at personal cost, and to remember the data that says that most men are on your side.

How a Combative Culture Can Lead to Silence

The climate of silence often is a product of a hypercompetitive and *combative workplace culture* in which value is attributed to dominating others in competition for power, authority, and status. In our survey of nearly 1,500 men in Canada, 46% of men were in organizations with a high level of combativeness.[11] In this type of workplace, employees are systematically encouraged to engage in stereotypically masculine practices and behaviors—the behaviors we discussed that create the man box—as a pathway to professional success.[12]

This workplace culture includes four defining behaviors:[13]

- **Show No Weakness:** The perception that showing emotion, raising doubts, or asking for advice is a sign of weakness and will not be respected.

  Example: A man pretends he knows how to complete a task he knows nothing about because he's worried that asking for help will make him seem weak.

- **Display Strength and Stamina:** The notion that characteristics such as physical size, athleticism, or ability to work long hours deserve admiration and respect in the workplace.

  Example: A male colleague insists on helping a woman professional courier whose job is to lift bags even though she can do her job without assistance and does not want his help.

- **Put Work First:** The belief that work must always come first, even before personal life and family.

  Example: Employees work late at night and on weekends, beyond their normal working hours, even during times when there is no true urgency, to demonstrate their commitment.

- **Perform with Dog-Eat-Dog Mentality:** A survival-of-the-fittest mindset; the belief that everyone should advocate only for themselves and not trust others.

  Example: A leader creates unhealthy competition among team members and demonstrates favoritism to those who align with the leader's view without question.

Other research has shown that this type of culture correlates with negative organizational dynamics such as poor workplace culture and toxic leadership; dominating coworker behaviors such as bullying and harassment; negative work attitudes among individuals such as burnout and greater intention to leave; and poor personal well-being including anxiety and depression.[14]

Our own findings reveal a direct link between a combative culture and the propensity to do nothing to interrupt sexism. When confronted by sexist behavior, 36% of men in more combative cultures report doing nothing compared to 6% of men in less combative cultures.[15]

The Climate of Silence Hurts Men Too

Did you notice that the traits that make up a climate of silence and combative cultures overlap with the characteristics of the man box? If you recall, the man box hurts everyone—including men themselves. When men are afraid to speak up in the face of sexism, both women and men suffer. Combative cultures and climates of silence become the water people swim in and are reinforced by employees across the board, intentionally or not, as "just the way things are around here." They become the unwritten rules for how to succeed in that organization, and deviating from those rules can feel like—and be—a real risk. Fear is natural, but silence maintains the status quo.

This is true beyond the corporate office. Frontline employees experience the climate of silence, as well. One man working in a frontline job told Alix Pollack of Catalyst that because of "the pressures to not be emotional, of not being able to be myself around everybody" when he feels depressed or sad, there is no "peaceful area" where he can truly express his emotions. That kind of safe space "almost doesn't exist [for] a man."

Another man in a frontline position poignantly told Pollack that if he were a light on a dimmer switch, he would not be able to turn his light "all the way up because no one actually cares." He questions whether anyone "honestly wants to know my truth, the experiences I've been through, especially as a Black man." He added, "You know, I don't think I've ever been my brightest self. I don't think I even know what I look like when I'm at my brightest, when my light is cranked up to 100. I've never seen that from myself."

The climate of silence can be devastating for everyone—women and men across all roles, levels, and industries. People in frontline roles working in spaces with a climate of silence, we discovered, experience high rates of gender-based hostility at work. Our research of nearly 4,500 employees across industries with frontline workers in Canada, the United Kingdom, and the United States reveals that 61% of women and 58% of men report experiencing gender-based hostility *within the past year*. An organizational climate of silence is a major driver of this type of behavior and is pervasive. Most frontline employees (89%) in this climate feel pressure to conform, leading to increased insults and hostility based on gender stereotypes.[16]

WHAT IS GENDER-BASED HOSTILITY?

Also known as "gender harassment," gender-based hostility shows up in two main ways: as sexist insults (such as comments that certain types of work are best suited for one gender and not another) and as crude comments (such as derogatory comments about a person's body, appearance, or sexual activity).[17] Examples include comments like, "A man in HR, you don't see that every day," and crude comments such as, "I know she is the expert here, but do we really want her to be onstage representing our company when she looks like that?"

Harassment and hostility—of women *and* men—festers within climates of silence in which employees believe they can't speak up about work-related problems because, if they do, they might experience negative consequences. Our data shows that gender-based hostility increases in frontline workplaces with higher levels of a climate of silence. Conversely, it also shows that when there is fair treatment in organizations, it reduces the climate of silence. When people see that their organizations value and practice fairness—offering equal access to promotion for both women and men, and treating employees fairly, free from the constraints of the man box and stereotypes about women, for example—they are more likely to feel empowered to speak up.

When Men Feel Speaking Up Isn't Worth It

When you work in a climate of silence and combativeness, you may very well feel a *sense of futility*—the belief that any efforts to make change will not matter or have the desired impact. Another word for it is hopelessness, a sense that it's not worth it because nothing will change anyway. Specifically, employees may doubt that managers will be receptive to the information they have to share, or they may feel that people in positions of power don't want to hear employee complaints or opinions, or they may believe they cannot effectively change the status quo.[18] As a senior leader in mining eloquently shared with us, "I didn't feel [psychologically] safe, and I didn't feel like there was any point . . . It felt like no matter what I did, nothing was going to change."[19]

In our survey, 45% of men indicated feeling high levels of futility related to speaking up against sexism. We also found a direct link between participants' perception of futility and their likelihood of doing nothing to interrupt sexism: 36% of men who reported a strong sense of futility said they would likely do nothing, whereas only 7% of men who didn't share that sense of futility said they would do nothing.[20]

As noted in the *Harvard Business Review*, "The desire to speak up is fundamentally about the wish to change something and make a difference. But, if you continue to cement employees' belief that speaking up is a waste of time, they'll save their breath."[21]

How Lack of Diversity and Inclusion Creates a Climate of Silence

What does a "climate of silence" look like on the ground? Again and again, corporate executives shared stories with me about past experiences with companies lacking meaningful diversity and inclusion. The result, they say, is chilling: Employees report feeling isolated and unable to speak their minds.

As a white man, Jim Fitterling is accustomed to being in corporate spaces where many, if not most, of the people around him look like him. But he is attuned to the challenges of being the "only" in the room—the one Black person, or gay person, or woman. He observes that for the "only," they may believe that they don't truly have a voice. He continues, "The expectations are high that you're going to bring in a different perspective. But at the same time, the barriers are very high. Let's say you bring in a new idea, and it gets shot down. And you do it again, and it gets shot down again. At a certain point, you may sense that you're being shut out of the discussion, and you might just give up."

At Dow, his goal is to have true diversity so that there's never a situation where someone feels that the only member of a traditionally underrepresented group is included just to "check a box." To crack through the climate of silence, he knows that teams must be truly diverse not just for the different ideas and perspectives people can bring but also to create an environment in which everyone feels safe speaking up and that all viewpoints can be shared, heard, and considered.

Christian, the global executive in Europe, has noticed the same thing. "I think it feels pretty lonely for a minority on a leadership team." He described an acquaintance who is the only woman on her executive team. "She was at a meeting recently and found that a woman board member was attending. She was relieved that there was someone else in the room who had shared experiences and perspectives." Having another woman in the room also meant that she could advance an alternate perspective without being "that woman" with her different ideas, and the representation of diversity in this way signaled that her voice would be welcomed and valued. You can't fix a climate of silence by merely adding bodies to the room to increase diversity—the environment and culture have to change too—but in this moment, for Christian's colleague, the climate of silence was lifted. One meeting at a time, one team at a time, this is how change happens.

But make no mistake, no matter how much diversity a team has in terms of representation, there remains the risk of a climate of silence unless the team demonstrates inclusion for everyone. Diversity must go beyond the optics of representation; it must be hardwired into the culture.

Francesco Del Porto of Barilla Group observes, "Earlier in my career, especially in sales, success was often tied to being the most competitive, assertive voice in the room. However, over time, I realized that those traits alone don't build strong, sustainable teams. At Barilla, we took a hard look at what we were rewarding: Were we promoting people because they were the loudest, or because they brought others along with them? We reviewed job descriptions, performance evaluations, and promotion criteria to ensure we were recognizing qualities like empathy, collaboration, and the ability to empower others.

"For me, it was about leading by example—demonstrating that listening, sharing credit, and making space for different voices isn't a 'soft' approach; it's how we achieve better results. Today, I'm proud that our leadership reflects those values. But we know this work is never done. We continually challenge ourselves to ensure our leaders represent the inclusive, balanced future we aspire to build."

Ron Carucci, cofounder and managing partner at Navalent, told me about a client he worked with years ago—a big global company that prided itself on its diverse leadership team. "They had a female Asian CEO and Black, Hispanic, lesbian, and gay team members. I listened to what they had to say so that I could begin my coaching work."

What he discovered on his first day on the job was that, despite the diversity of identities, there was no diversity of thought or ideas. "I told them, 'Here are five times you had an opportunity to engage with different perspectives. But your responses were those of a team looking to avoid diverse thinking, not embrace it.' I heard the statements of a group hiding behind its diverse representation and trying to protect its homogeneity."

Ron believes that boards and senior leaders must play a large role in determining their organizational culture, and they need to ensure that inclusion is coupled with diversity. "If I'm sitting on a board and someone tells me they've increased their female quotient by X percent in one quarter, my response is: 'Let's ask the women what *their* experience is. How do they feel in meetings? What are their salaries like? Why do they leave? And, which of their ideas are being heard and champi-oned?'" Hiring people just to fill certain demographic boxes actually reduces inclusion. Instead, to ensure true change so that everyone reaps the benefits of an inclusive workplace, you need to build a workplace culture that actively seeks to include not just different identities but ideas, experiences, and ways of working.

Breaking the Silence

Silence is fantastic when you're at the movie theater or library. But in the workplace, you *want* noise because you don't want anyone to believe that speaking up will hurt their career.

When employees feel pressured to be silent . . .

- bad behavior is tolerated and may be seen as endorsed by leadership;
- no one shares minority or unpopular opinions, even if they're helpful; and
- employees who are targeted and harassed feel marginalized.

Even when sexism is unintentional, it's still important for us to speak out against it so it doesn't become normalized as part of the culture.

The same is true for the man box. We need to encourage men to come to work as their authentic selves, just as we are encouraging women to do the same. For the best outcomes in employees' health, engagement, job performance, and intent to stay, we need to reject silence and embrace the positive noise that comes with disrupting outdated gender expectations and creating workplace cultures that benefit us all.

PART TWO
The Solution

In Part 1, I laid out the problem: Societal norms and expectations of how men and women are supposed to behave harm everyone, and no one can do their best work under these circumstances. Men and women alike are constrained by the behaviors we have been taught are "acceptable" for our respective genders, and organizations are put at risk because these narrow expectations of both men and women, combined with underrepresentation of women at senior levels, have a financial cost. The good news is that men *want* to be gender partners, breaking down the "man box" that limits them and creating environments that support everyone thriving in the workplace.

In Part 2, I offer the solution: the Catalyst roadmap to gender partnership. It is designed for men and women managers, senior leaders, and executives who are interested in stepping up as gender partners and seeking practical and tactical guidance to show them how. We call them the 5 B's of gender partnership:

1. Begin with You
2. Break Down What's Not Working
3. Build Up What's in It for Men
4. Bridge the Gender Gaps
5. Bring Humanity to Work

Following the 5 B's enables you to reflect on how you can be an agent of change; break free of gender norms that aren't serving you or your teams; show the men at your organization how they benefit from gender partnership; and cocreate a culture that celebrates and supports our uniqueness and connection across gender. In Part 1, I laid out the business case for change. Part 2 will demonstrate how you can enact change by using the Catalyst roadmap. We offer examples from leaders and organizations we hold up as best practice examples. The men and women you will get to know in the following pages show by their actions that we all have the power to create workplace cultures in which men and women alike can thrive.

Let's get started.

5

Begin with You

5 B's of Gender Partnership

- ⊘ **Begin with You**
- ○ Break Down What's Not Working
- ○ Build Up What's in It for Men
- ○ Bridge the Gender Gaps
- ○ Bring Humanity to Work

Being a gender partner is not something you can do without having some skin in the game. I encourage you to start with reflection so when the time comes, you're primed to use your voice and influence to make change.

Lynne Thompson, an aerospace industry and engineering leader, worked at the Boeing Company for nearly four decades. When she was hired for her first executive position in the 1990s as the 747 aircraft systems chief engineer, she saw that thousands of hours of electrical work were being poured into each plane for customer requests, such as the installation of video screens on the backs of seats. Yet it was clear to her that much of the work being done involved correcting errors with unnecessary labor and expense.

Confused, she approached the electrical leader and asked what was going on. He broke down all the steps involved for getting the engineering work finalized, and Lynne quickly realized the electrical team was being brought in too late in the process, forcing them to redo steps that already had been completed. Lynne put an end to this inefficiency. She reviewed the steps being taken and shared information about each step with everyone involved. She brought everyone together to have a conversation about fixing the problem. Once everyone had visibility of what others were doing, the entire process shifted and became streamlined.

"Within a matter of weeks," Lynne told me on a video call, "everything got caught up. Suddenly, electrical hours went from 20,000 to 30,000 per airplane down to under 5,000 hours. Now, they were getting their work right the first time. It was a huge breakthrough." Lynne was able to achieve this breakthrough because she asked questions and listened to input from everyone in the system . . . but the groundwork for this type of leadership behavior had been laid years before.

Lynne attributes her ability to conquer this challenge to a mindset instilled in her by the former Boeing Commercial Aircraft CEO Alan Mulally, who later became the CEO of Ford Motor Company. The two had worked closely earlier in his career when he had been the vice president of engineering. Alan had demonstrated the power of information sharing and the pitfalls of keeping different teams separated in isolated silos. When people understand how everything works together, they are empowered to make good decisions.

"What I saw during the time I worked with Alan was that he wanted people to share information about the state of the business," Lynne reflected. "Alan wanted us to bring in the data. He would say, 'The data will set you free.' It was not about pointing fingers. It was about saying, 'Hey, I've discovered this problem; this part of the organization is out of control, but it's not their fault. It's because they're getting fed the information they need late.' By working together and being transparent, we made everyone's jobs easier."

Alan also offered to sponsor Lynne after a colleague introduced them. Lynne recalls entering his office: "There was a lot going on; Alan was getting nonstop calls from an airline. But he sat down with me, and we had this really kind conversation, and he got to know my background. Then he asked, 'Would it be okay if I shared your profile in my talent team meeting? If more leaders are familiar with your background, you could have more opportunities at Boeing.'"

Alan, in short, provided Lynne with an opportunity that had previously seemed closed to her. Now the door was open, and she stepped into it. With Alan's sponsorship, she was recognized, and when positions became available, she started appearing on candidate lists.

What Lynne experienced is an example of what Catalyst calls *gender partnership*. As described earlier in this book, gender partnership is when men and women assume mutual accountability for advancing fairness and inclusion and work together to create culture change for the benefit of everyone. Gender partners engage in this work both within and across lines of gender (i.e., women partnering with women, men partnering with men, and men and women partnering with each other). To be clear, this is not about a man stepping in to solve a problem *for* a woman. And it is not about "fixing" women. But it's also not about fixing men. It is about all people leaning into empathy, active listening, and collaborative problem-solving to improve psychological safety (where employees feel comfortable taking risks and making mistakes)[1] and belonging and, importantly, to help close gender gaps.

Alan Mulally never said, "I'm going to handpick Lynne and make her a superstar." Even though he never thought of himself as one, Alan was a true gender partner because he saw incredible talent in Lynne and ensured that her talents were seen, her voice was heard, and she had opportunities to shine.

The rest was history: Lynne climbed the executive ranks at Boeing, and by the time she retired in 2025, she was Vice President and General Manager of Engineering Strategy and Operations. Alan's leadership was transformational for culture and for productivity. He operated as a gender partner and modeled it for others. In doing so, he was proactive in making space for Lynne to bring her natural skills and talents as a problem-solver, collaborator, and empathetic leader to a workplace that had been trained to appreciate these behaviors rather than discount them as the "soft skills of female leadership."

I share this story to illustrate the first of Catalyst's "5 B's" that can help solve the problem of gender gaps at your organization: Begin with You.

Use Your Voice and Influence

This step is critical because while women have made incredible progress in the workplace, we can't do it alone. Historically, women advocated for themselves and for other women. From the 1930s to the 1970s, attitudes about women working changed, with greater acceptance of women of all backgrounds serving in the labor force. Increasingly, married women pursued higher education and began the precarious challenge of managing their jobs both inside and outside the home, while many other women, including those lacking formal career education, have always worked outside the home.[2] With this new model in place, women became increasingly vocal about the need for pay equity and fair treatment at work.[3]

More recently, as activism around gender inequality has grown, men have shown that they want to be more involved as *allies* who join in the work of promoting "women's issues."[4]

Male allies are important, but to change attitudes and behaviors, we need *partners* who are focused on mutual accountability.[5] With men as allies, women are positioned as the only beneficiaries of this activism; the dynamic is unidirectional. Similarly, the agenda of men's allyship is largely if not wholly set by others, not the men themselves; the job of male allies is to support, not orchestrate.[6] Being the male executive sponsor of a women's employee resource group (ERG), for example, is allyship behavior. The work is largely driven by women and for women, and the role of the ally is to offer funding, visibility, credibility, and more. Allyship is critical and has a necessary and impactful place in this work, but it is not enough to change the culture on a larger scale. It was this realization that propelled us at Catalyst to conceptualize gender partnership, and it is the reason I am writing this book. If we want to change the outcome, we must be willing to rethink the process.

If we want systemic change, not just incremental change, we need another approach. With gender partnership, everyone sets the agenda for change, and everyone does the work of accomplishing it. Accountability is shared by everyone, and the benefits are reaped by everyone. This is why men partnering with other men to advance their own learning, share best practices, and support each other in breaking out of the man box is an example of gender partnership just as much as a man interrupting exclusionary behavior toward a woman colleague. In short, while *allyship* focuses on the benefits of men's support for women, *gender partnership* is about everyone being both agents and beneficiaries of systemic change, closing gender gaps to drive fairness and inclusion for all.

Dow Chair and CEO Jim Fitterling models this accountability. He makes the Dow ambition to become "the most innovative, customer-centric, inclusive, and sustainable material sciences company in the world" a mantra. "Jim repeats this ambition all the time," Amy Wilson, general counsel and corporate secretary for Dow, told me. "And everybody knows it. Every employee can recite it. We'll all start laughing because we can all say it together." She explains why the mantra is so significant: It reiterates that Dow has inclusive values that align to their ambition and that everything at Dow is anchored to this statement.

In other words, Dow's business strategy is rooted in inclusion, and everyone is expected to live it. Every time I have been in Jim's presence, I've observed personally how he embodies inclusion in both words and actions. He is among the first to respond to requests for support in leveraging his network to advance Catalyst's mission. And he ensures the women on Dow's leadership team, including COO Karen S. Carter and general counsel and corporate secretary Amy Wilson, share the company's spotlight, like leading on our Catalyst advisory board and sharing their stories for this book.

How can men make this shift from ally or advocate to gender partner, as Jim does? It starts with you, and the awareness that the influence you carry as a man in the workplace can be a force for change.

Make Yourself Visible

On paper, gender partnership is a beautiful concept. But let's face it: Leaders like Alan Mulally and Jim Fitterling have never been the norm in the workplace. Besides, for gender partnership to work, we can't just cultivate individuals to take on this work; we need to create work environments in which mutual accountability is the oxygen everyone breathes. That is precisely why Catalyst initiated our first MARC learning programs in 2016—to support and encourage people to act both on the individual level and, if they are empowered to do so, on an organizational level.

I sought out Ron Carucci to learn more about the behaviors of male leaders committed to gender partnership. The cofounder of Navalent, Ron works with CEOs and executives pursuing transformational change for their organizations, leaders, and industries—so he has his finger on the pulse of influential organizational leaders.

Ron is also a member of a group called White Men for Racial Justice (WMRJ), whose website declares, "Our shared vision is an America in which everyone feels valued, has access to equitable resources to reach their full potential, and is part of diverse, joyful communities."[7] When I learned about Ron's passion and purpose to convene white men to support the advancement of underrepresented groups, I wanted his specific thoughts on how to engage men in enacting change.

"After the police murder of George Floyd in 2020," Ron told me on a video call, "two friends of mine started the group because they saw all the protests in the street and noticed that participants were almost all non-white men. They wondered: 'Where are all the white guys? You know, we've played a disproportionate role in making the playing field unlevel. We should play a disproportionate role in making it better.' I attended an early meeting right after they formed and fell in love with this community."

Ron strongly believes that men *want* to step up as gender partners but have not yet gotten to the point of being confident in knowing *how* to step up. "There are a lot of us out there, hiding in the shadows," he told me.

He explained that through his work with WMRJ he has learned that, as a group, white men need to learn how to belong. So many have been conditioned to be competitive, to be emotionally stoic and appear confident, to get out there and fight, and to see the world as a zero-sum game. They've been conditioned to control the belonging of others while never experiencing the feelings of deep belonging that come from being an equal among others—the kinds of belonging you might see among women or among people belonging to the same racial or ethnic groups. "When [the men] get a taste of this connection, you watch this light go on," said Ron. "They realize, 'This is what I have been missing. I didn't know how to find it. I didn't know it was even okay to want it.'"

Whereas MARC programs are designed for a mixed-gender audience, WMRJ encourages men-only discussion groups. Ron said that having women or other underrepresented groups in the room during these intimate conversations puts men on guard. They feel they can't be vulnerable.

"The experience of letting down one's guard and being human and flawed and imperfect and uncertain" is an important first step for many white men, he continued. "Once they've tasted the experience of full acceptance and no judgment and care, and of truly belonging and being known and seen, they can then know how to look for that experience in other types of identities and groups and, more importantly, to use their influence and positions of power to ensure those experiences are created for others."

Once this barrier is broken and the competitive, zero-sum-game approach is revealed as a sham, men are primed to see that workplace practices, policies, and systems should be built to ensure fair opportunity for all employees, and that treating men and women differently in all aspects of the workplace—recruitment, retention, development, and advancement—is unfair and wrong.

Reflect on Your Own Experiences

Being a gender partner means making workplaces more inclusive for everyone, including men. Yet many men have trouble seeing outside of the box—after all, this is the only reality that many have ever known.

So it should come as no surprise—as we learned in one of our very first research projects when we began studying partnerships between men and women—that a key determinant of whether or not men will advocate for women is having a strong sense of fair play. And a strong sense of fair play is directly related to having experienced discrimination themselves.[8] For some men, having this personal experience enables them to look inward, reflect on their own lives, and better put themselves in the shoes of their women colleagues.

For example, one of the men in frontline positions we've interviewed told Alix Pollack that he had experienced sexual harassment at work. He said, "I was a server at a restaurant in New Jersey, and at the end of my shift, a coworker came over and, I hate to say it, but she slapped me on the butt, and I was in complete and utter shock. And I was thinking, did I do or say anything to invite this?"

"How did that feel to have that reaction?" Alix asked.

"I hated it," he answered. "I really did. And in that moment, I felt violated. I was really upset." He added, "And I don't like the fact that I questioned myself, like, 'What did I do?' I don't like the fact that I had to go through that series of questions with myself, because I didn't do anything [wrong]."

Alix asked if he thought his response influenced the way he now thinks about women's stories of sexual harassment.

"Yes, absolutely," he told her. "It makes me much more empathetic and much more sensitive when women are sharing these stories because you know that the second that you share a similar story, you're going to be seen in a different light." He reflected on the shame and self-doubt he felt, and the judgment he placed on himself for "making trouble" by saying something, even though logically he knew it wasn't his fault and that speaking up was the right thing to do. These reflections, he said, made him think differently about what it must be like for women in similar situations. As he put it, "In your mind you run this idea that maybe you'll be seen as a troublemaker, as someone who's rocking the boat just for the sake of rocking the boat. Someone who's being sensitive to maybe something that didn't really happen. So yeah, it was a huge, huge eye opener."

Similarly, at a recent MARC training, a middle-aged white man shared that when he's at home in the US, he never feels discriminated against—and doesn't even think about discrimination because it's just not part of his reality. But when he travels abroad for work assignments, especially in countries where English is not the native language, it's a different story. Outside the US, he experiences being an "other" who does not fit in and is looked at sometimes with suspicion. "I know they're thinking, 'Why can't he learn our language? Why doesn't he select the local delicacies from the menu?' And those are totally fair questions! The reality is that even when I do try, it's still really obvious that I'm an outsider."

Many women feel "othered" at work on a regular basis, even though they're not outsiders. Women of color experience "othering" at even higher rates. Many white men may experience being "othered" only on occasion,[9] but I hope the sensation impacts them enough to empathize with colleagues experiencing this dynamic frequently.

Stay Open to Ideas and Build Trust

Managers are among the important forces for positive change in building gender partnership within your organization, given their role in shaping employees' overall work experience. When employees perceive that their manager is open to hearing different ideas, it creates an inclusive environment and decreases the risk of developing climates of silence. Our research on over 2,000 men in Europe finds that 62% of men experiencing high levels of manager openness—feeling that their manager is open to hearing and considering their ideas—are likely to directly interrupt sexist comments in the workplace. Meanwhile, only 35% of men who report low levels of manager openness would do so.[10]

If you are scratching your head and wondering how these two seemingly unrelated things—a manager being open to hearing and acting upon employee ideas and an employee speaking up in the face of sexism—are connected, let's get a little deeper. Negin Sattari, one of the researchers who conducted the study that produced the report *When Managers Are Open, Men Feel Heard and Interrupt Sexism*, explained, "Our research found that managers who are open to employee ideas can contribute to environments where men are encouraged to speak up in the face of sexist comments. Part of this effect was driven by the positive impact of manager openness and, more broadly, on the sense of feeling heard at work."[11]

Manager openness also leads to building trust on your teams, by creating an environment in which people feel safe speaking up and supported in their work. As Telva McGruder, executive director of Global Body Manufacturing Engineering at General Motors, looks back on her 30-plus years at GM, she recalls several male colleagues and leaders who supported and advocated for women through openness and trust. One in particular—Dane Parker—stands out as an example of how men can be transformative gender partners.

"I met Dane in 2016 while interviewing for an executive position," Telva says. "Even before I was hired, Dane's ability to connect with other people was evident. As we worked together over the following years, I noted that Dane purposefully and proactively used his position to promote gender equity."

She recalls, "My second day on the job, Dane copied me on an email to a supplier who had requested a meeting. He wrote, *Hey, thanks for your interest in meeting with me. I've got a fantastic engineering leader on board. Her name is Telva McGruder. I've copied her on this message. She will answer any questions that you have and help guide you in the right direction.*

"This was on day two! Clearly, I didn't know what the heck was going on. I had just gotten there! But from the moment I showed up, Dane demonstrated—not only to me, but to everyone interacting with him—that he believed in me. That doesn't happen very often.

"And it was consistent," she adds. "When it happened the first time, I thought, *Oh, that's cool.* And then it kept happening again and again. By virtue of building these relationships, I built my skill and my judgment. I'd share my thoughts with Dane. He'd challenge my thinking, and we'd have fantastic conversations. I never felt like I worked *for* him. I worked *with* him."

Dane continued to develop and support Telva by advocating for her in spaces where she didn't already have a seat at the table. "As I was building my capability and demonstrating it to Dane, he started sponsoring me in forums that he was in," she says. "I know this because he told me. I didn't have to go to him and say, 'Will you be my sponsor?'

"For example, if Dane was sponsoring me for a particular stretch opportunity and he got feedback like, *Well, we don't know her,* he would begin building a bridge. 'Let me help you with that. Telva, this is Joe. Joe, this is Telva. I want you to get to know her because she has these skills, and you complement each other. Telva, this is what I love about Joe. Joe, here is what I like about Telva. Y'all build a relationship because you will love each other too.'"

While being a connector was part of Dane's personality, Telva points out that he was also committed to using his position with intent. "Dane's mission was to uplift women in the company, and men too. He looked at people's skills and capabilities to make decisions on who he would actively open doors for. He did that proactively, equitably, and with purpose.

"Because of the work Dane did, I became a senior executive at General Motors," she shares. "But it wasn't because he was just picking some woman. He had high expectations of me, which is exactly what I needed because that's what I respond to."

It all started with Dane's trust in Telva, which enabled Telva to build her confidence and credibility.

Be Vulnerable

Francesco Del Porto of Barilla Group says, "There was a time when I believed that showing vulnerability as a leader might be perceived as weakness. Now, I realize that being open fosters trust. When I share my own struggles and show emotions, it encourages others to do the same. This is how we build a culture of support, not just for women, but for everyone. I hold myself to this standard every day. If I expect my team to be honest and open, I must lead by example."

Likewise, Dow Chair and CEO Jim Fitterling is honest and vulnerable about who he is. Yet, for many years, he felt he needed to hide a key part of his identity: He is gay. He was with the company for 30 years before he came out. Here is his story:

I joined Dow in 1984, and at that time in the corporate world, it just wasn't a thing to be open and out. There were different norms, different sets of rules. But years later, I had a bout with stage-four cancer and had to go through surgery and chemo. It was a soul-searching time for me, and I reflected on several things while I was going through recovery. And one of them was how to eliminate some stressors in my life. Leading two separate lives, one of them hidden, was a huge stressor.

The cancer scare was one aspect of it. The other aspect of it was that I was close to being named Chief Operating Officer. I realized that employees were looking to me for leadership. And if I wasn't out openly, what did that say about me? What did that say about the company? I felt that having this visibility was another reason to come out.

So, with the help of a lot of people, after I had come out to my team, I decided to come out in a public forum. It was a webcast for 53,000 employees on Coming Out Day.

The response was overwhelmingly positive, like 99-plus percent positive. The board was supportive; I spoke with each one of them individually beforehand and every single one said, "Good for you. It's the right thing to do; I'm proud of you for doing it." And the employees were also supportive.

But more than the responses from individuals was the change in company culture. We had lifted a lid on a conversation that we hadn't had, couldn't have had, until that time—at the top of the organization. It was a turning point when things began to change for the company and the community. I think I made it okay to talk openly about being gay and what some of the challenges are and why people choose to stay in the closet versus coming out. It's been beneficial for me, and I think for other people at Dow. My only regret is that I didn't do it sooner.

I was intrigued by Jim's choice of words: that he had "lifted the lid." For women and people of color, your identity within those groups is often visible and obvious. Gay people, however, can often shield that part of their identity. Being openly gay can, for some people, mean removing the lid that is covering and hiding them, allowing them to be their whole selves, and doing so is usually easier when that person trusts the surrounding culture to include and support them.

Lifting the lid is a core component for real change. Jim explains,[12]

After my bout with cancer and my coming out, I saw life differently. You can't avoid progress on certain things because they're scary or challenging. That's why, when I became CEO of Dow in 2018, we made our ambition to become the most innovative, customer-centric, inclusive, and sustainable materials science company in the world. A big part of delivering on a goal like that is believing you can do it—just like believing life will be better after coming out, or you can beat cancer. Fear isn't going to help, and it may actually accelerate defeat. To do this, we know we need everyone working together and focused on the challenges in front of us. We need to make sure no one fears being their whole self while they're at work—because we need everyone's inputs included to achieve our goals. Every day we try to ensure that our people have a safe environment at work.

We aim to recruit and retain the best talent possible. And we've done a great job of that. We hire our people because they are the best, and because we value their inputs—all of them. I know what it's like to spend energy and mindshare hiding who I am. It can affect your ability to contribute. Part of you, sometimes all of you, goes into a shell. You withdraw. Helping ensure people can be themselves empowers them. It allows people to contribute fully. And, as a result, it empowers the entire organization and helps us achieve our goals.

Be a Vocal Advocate for Women

Christian Conti is an incredible gender partner who is constantly strategizing how to publicly recognize the women he worked with in his prior role as managing vice president at Gartner, an information services company. He leverages his LinkedIn platform to do shout-outs of these women. Why does he do this? Because he recognizes that it's the right thing to do, it's the smart thing to do, and he has the platform and influence that allows him to do so.

"Having a platform is a privilege. When I post something on LinkedIn and get 10,000 or 20,000 views, that definitely feeds my ego and gives me a dopamine hit. But it also raises the question: What do I want to say that's worthy of the time of thousands of people in my network? What values do I want to communicate?"

For Christian, the answer is shining a light on women's excellence. And he regards himself as singularly positioned to advocate for women because of his identity as a white man. "It's like you've got all this influence just overflowing out of your pocket." He jokes, "I'm like a piñata stuffed with privilege." But then he gets serious. "As male leaders and executives, we build all this equity, and then what are we doing with it? If you have generated credibility over the course of your career, and then you're not using it, what have you built that reputation for? I think that when you achieve a level of success, you really have an obligation to send the elevator back down for somebody else."

Here's where accountability comes in. Not only does Christian use his platform to raise awareness about specific women he knows, and about women in general; he also *prods other men to do the same thing*. He looks for ways to get other men to recognize any advantages they may have and then leverage them to be more inclusive.

Does he directly confront men and tell them to be more inclusive? No—that is the wrong approach, he says. Instead, *and this is genius*, he creates a sense of FOMO (fear of missing out) about working with women. By highlighting the benefits that women have brought to him and his business, Christian provokes other men in positions where they have a say over who gets hired or promoted at their company to acknowledge, "I want that too!" He shared with me one recent example.

I had a young guy on my team that we promoted to sales manager. I have this tradition where after someone's first year as manager, I take them out to a nice dinner and talk about what's to come over the next couple of years, and what I think they're capable of.

So we're at dinner, having the conversations I always have, and about halfway through, he said, "I appreciate you pushing me. And I want to talk to you about something. You know, I've been reading your LinkedIn posts all year. I really respect who you are as a person and a leader. I'm 12 years into my career at Gartner and I have never worked for a woman before. I feel like I'm missing something."

I had created this FOMO [through my LinkedIn posts], which was much more constructive than telling a guy, "Hey, you need to invest more in women." I turn it around and tell people the ways that women elevate my business and career. And guys are listening to me, as, at this point, I have built up a certain level of respect. And they're thinking, *This is somebody who's happy and successful and talking so much about the role women have played in his career. Why don't I have that?* It's such a human instinct to think: *Wait, you have something I don't have. I want it.*

With permission from Christan and Inna Gardner, group vice president of Gartner, as well as Caroline Ritter, senior advisor at TPG, I'm sharing two LinkedIn conversations initiated by Christian—both of which generated hundreds of comments and thousands of views—to demonstrate what exceptional gender partnership looks like.[13]

Christian Conti (he/him) ✓ · 3rd+   + Follow ···
Experienced Sales Leader Turned Unplugged Globetrotter 🌐
10mo · 🌐

This edition of Female Leaders who've inspired and impacted me is especially close to my heart 🖤

For nearly a quarter century Inna Gardner has been a role model, a mentor, a partner and most importantly a best friend.

As our careers have grown side by side, I'm constantly in awe of the incredible work she's done to build her businesses at Gartner, raise two incredible children, and be constantly generous with her time and attention to help others.

Things I've learned from Inna:

1. Authenticity Over Everything- what you see is what you get with Inna, and what you get is intelligence, humor and a constant desire to make things better.

2. Grace Under Pressure- we've been through it all (at work and personally), and I'm always in awe of Inna's ability to stay calm and focused and to always move everyone around her forward with her head held high.

3. Be a People Leader First- No one who has worked with Inna has ever felt anything less than seen and appreciated. She puts her people and her partners first, and she's consistently investing in the incredible talent that surrounds her.

4. Send the Elevator Back Down- Inna advocates. For female sellers and leaders. For LGBTQIA+ colleagues. For increasing diversity and inclusion in every possible and her people legacy demonstrates that clearly.

In short, she's pretty freaking amazing. And I feel lucky every single day that's she's my ride or die no matter what's happening at work or at home 🏡

If you've been lucky enough to have had a little Inna magic in your life, shout down below! 👇

Jennifer McCollum ✅ · 3rd+   (edited) 10mo ···
CEO | Author | International Speaker | Gender Equity Advocate | L...

Love everything about this post and the swarm of response in support! What a great example of lifting up incredible women leaders! Thanks Christian Conti (he/him) and Inna Gardner - you are both fabulous!

Like · ♥ 1 | Reply · 1 reply

Christian Conti (he/him) ✅ `Author`   10mo ···
Experienced Sales Leader Turned Unplugged Globetrotter 🌐

Jennifer McCollum I wouldn't be here without incredible female role models and friend alike you and inna!

Like · ♥ 1 | Reply

And a second example to carry the point home:

Christian Conti (he/him) ✅ · 3rd+   **+ Follow** ···
Experienced Sales Leader Turned Unplugged Globetrotter 🌐
8mo · 🌐

Women Who Inspire Me, Quarter Century Work Wife Edition 💅

Caroline Ritter has been a mentor, a best friend and a true ride or die for over two decades. Wickedly smart, endlessly wise and warm, adventurous and curious, she's inspired more careers than I could ever hope to count.

Things Caroline has taught me:

➡️ Fear Your Comfort Zone-Caroline thrives in uncertainty. New roles, new domains, new skills, new companies, new geographies. Her example and advice is one of the reasons I made it to London 🇬🇧

➡️ Your Network Is Your Net Worth-Caroline consistently invests is growing and caring for her personal and professional networks Small gestures of care, checking in, making powerful connections without expecting anything back, she's an iconic example
Of what authentic networking looks like.

➡️ Foul Weather Friends Are Priceless- Caroline always shows up for people, in ways big and small. And when things get tough she just leans in harder to support those around her. It's hardly an exaggeration to say she's been through my darkest days with me and I'll never forget it.

I know my LinkedIn must be filled with people who're better for knowing Caroline, make some noise 🔊

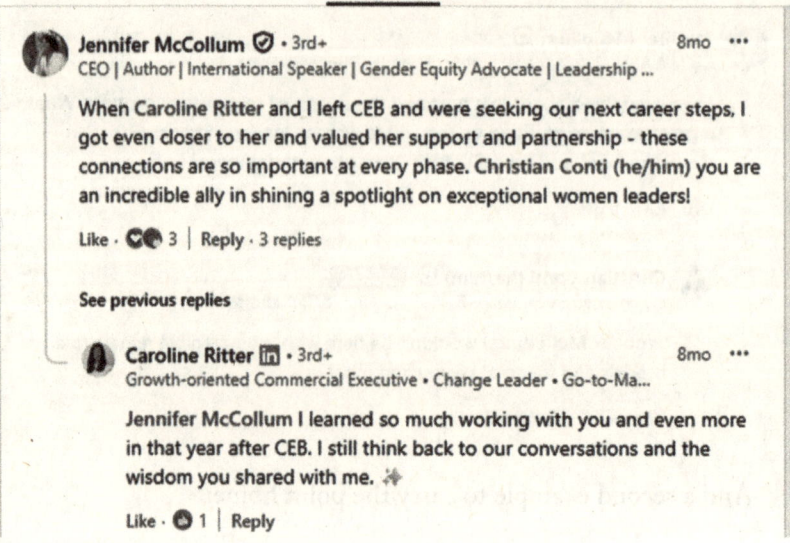

Christian demonstrates with his words and actions that gender partnership is not just the right thing to do. It's not just the smart thing to do. It's also the thing that most people *want* to do.

6

Break Down What's Not Working

5 B's of Gender Partnership

- ⊘ Begin with You
- ⊘ **Break Down What's Not Working**
- ○ Build Up What's in It for Men
- ○ Bridge the Gender Gaps
- ○ Bring Humanity to Work

Not everything is broken, but some things are—such as stereo-types, harmful or misguided assumptions, and outdated leader-ship norms that aren't serving anyone. Part of making progress is letting go of the things we need to leave behind.

We have seen that many workplace cultures are set up in ways that block women's opportunities and progress,[1] along with men's ability to show up authentically as themselves.[2] Clearly, we need to fix what's broken. In the stories that follow, leaders share how they discovered what was holding back inclusion in their own workplaces and what they did to break the barriers.

Spoiler alert: Rigid gender norms about how women and men should behave can hinder our efforts to create inclusive workplaces where everyone is given the opportunity to thrive. It's time to explore how our expectations and stereotypes drive our assumptions and beliefs—and be open to new ways of thinking and working.

Say Goodbye to "Command and Control"

Alan Mulally has famously rejected a traditionally masculine style of leadership. The former CEO of Ford and Boeing Commercial Aircraft is the first to acknowledge that he is not a "command and control" leader by nature. "It's not who I am," he told me. "It's not how I want to be treated, and it's not how I can be the best contributor."

Alan came about his leadership style naturally: His parents instilled values in him as a young child that taught him to work together with others and see the value and potential in everyone. He often quotes the mantras his parents repeated daily as he left the house: "Now remember, Alan . . .

- "The purpose of life is to love and be loved, in that order."
- "Seek to understand before seeking to be understood."
- "It's nice to be important, but more important to be nice."
- "By working together with others, you can make the most positive contribution to the most people."

When he entered the working world, however, these were not the values he saw being modeled. Instead, he saw successful leaders—almost exclusively men—simply telling team members what to do. So, earlier in his career as a leader, Alan believed he needed to be more like them to succeed, and he tried to emulate the style that was so counter to his upbringing.

A few things happened as a result. First, people stopped sharing things openly for fear of retribution. They didn't feel safe.

Second, his staff didn't like his top-down, non-collaborative leadership style. The pilots of the airplanes and members of the engineering team came to see him and said, "Alan, if you keep doing this, we're going to quit. We know your inclination is to work cooperatively, so stop trying to be someone else."

Around this time, in the late 1980s, Frank Shrontz was early in his tenure as chair of Boeing,[3] and he knew Alan well. He called Alan to his office and said, "I believe in you and in your collaborative leadership style; do not change that. I know you're dealing with a lot of people who are not like you, but keep being who you truly are. I can see you taking on more responsibility as a result."

Alan reverted back to his core, to what he now calls his "Working Together Leadership & Management System,"[4] and regained the support from his direct reports and his leaders. Everyone experienced the benefit. He launched the Boeing 777 under Shrontz's leadership, and every time he was promoted and introduced to a new team, he brought his values and his system that created clear expectations of the operating process and behaviors of all leaders.

Here are the leadership principles and practices Alan has used to lead his companies, his boards, and even his family. Most notable to me is how they align to the characteristics of a fair and inclusive workplace, in which everyone can feel a sense of belonging. It is no surprise that the culture he has created in every team has resulted in exceptional business performance.

OUR "WORKING TOGETHER": PRINCIPLES, PRACTICES, AND CONNECTED, COLLABORATIVE & ALIGNED CULTURE OF LOVE BY DESIGN

OUR OPERATING PROCESSES AND EXPECTED BEHAVIORS
SKILLED, HEALTHY, PSYCHOLOGICALLY SAFE, AND MOTIVATED TEAMS

- People first...Love 'em up ♥
- Everyone is included
- Compelling vision, comprehensive strategy, and relentless, positive implementation
- Clear performance goals
- One plan
- Facts and data

- Expect the unexpected and expect to deal with it
- Everyone knows the plan, the status, and areas that need special attention
- Propose a plan, positive, "find-a-way" attitude
- Respect, listen, help, and appreciate each other
- Emotional resilience, trust the process and each other
- Have fun — enjoy the journey and each other

PGA ♥
Profitable Growth for All
CREATING VALUE AND GROWTH FOR ALL THE STAKEHOLDERS AND THE GREATER GOOD

© 2025 Alan Mulally

Would you ever have expected the CEO of huge, successful corporations like Ford and Boeing to include heart emojis and a smiley face on a business slide? Alan saw that members of his team loved working on the 777 and F150, but they needed a model to guide the way teams worked together, leading with behaviors like inclusion, love, and collaboration. This approach fostered leaders who showed their humanity and included everyone. And it became clear to employees at these iconic American companies that these principles not only helped the companies soar but were also beneficial outside of the workplace in every aspect of life. I encourage you to create a version of these expectations for your team as well.

I asked Alan to reflect on how he can serve as an example for other leaders, and he said, "I've seen it both ways, and by doing it *this* way, with my 'working together' system and principles, we could always do more good if we grew the company and people."

Question Assumptions

"You're one of the most talented sales leaders I've ever worked with. If you weren't gay, I could see you eventually becoming the CEO."

It's been twenty years since these words were said to a man I'll call Martin, who was at that time an executive at a global information services company. But even now, two decades later, he remembers the incident vividly. Martin had just been promoted to managing director, the youngest person ever at his company to hold that role, and his sponsor took him out to dinner to celebrate. As they were enjoying their entrées, his sponsor said those memorable words—probably thinking he was paying Martin a compliment.

Martin reflected to me, "He told me I should feel proud of myself, and that I had worked so hard and earned this promotion." But in the same breath, he insulted Martin as a human being. "In a moment like that," Martin told me, "you can stay quiet and let it defeat you, or you can allow your anger to motivate you to change things." Martin did go on to be highly successful at his company, but even decades later, he hasn't forgotten the pain of being in the position where he felt he had to stay silent. "I chose not to speak up. This guy was responsible for my career. He was my advocate. So I said nothing. And I stayed collegial with him for many years."

Martin's sponsor communicated overt bias against gay employees. In using the words "If you weren't gay," he named his discrimination and brought it out into the open. Moreover, his statement was not only a commentary about Martin being "different" from the norm, and "different" from the image of the typical CEO—it was also an observation about their company's work culture: It had a narrow and non-inclusive vision of leadership, and those who did not conform would not advance.

Part of what shocked me about this story was that Martin's sponsor said it out loud and without hesitation. Most of the bias I see in workplaces is not typically so open. Often, people's biases can differ from their expressed beliefs without them realizing it. In fact, anyone can operate under the influence of implicit (sometimes called unconscious) bias—including leaders.[5] Implicit bias refers to unconscious attitudes, stereotypes, and beliefs that influence our beliefs and actions without our conscious awareness.

Here's an example: Previously, I talked about Alan Mulally and the role he played in breaking down a deep-rooted assumption at Boeing some 30 years ago. Lynne Thompson, who worked for Boeing then, entered the company at a time when women had to wait and hope that an executive tapped her to become a manager—even though she was eminently qualified. This "wait your turn" culture was unintentionally biased against women because leadership at Boeing at that time was dominated by men, who were more apt to recognize people like themselves as already qualified for leadership roles.

One of the common ways implicit bias shows up in workplaces is the tendency to gravitate toward people similar to ourselves and avoid those who are different. Called the "affinity bias," it can result in leaders hiring and promoting people who share the leader's same gender, race, age, or educational background, even when equally or more talented people are available. While most leaders operate this way without intention or realization, it discriminates against people who are seen as different.[6]

Why do some underlying assumptions and preconceived notions have staying power? Because they are "invisible forces," says Tonya Matthews, CEO of the International African American Museum and a leader in the global movement to empower the imagination and careers of women and girls in STEM (science, technology, engineering, and math). Because implicit bias is invisible, "no amount of objective business-case data will change the existing structures," she told me when I interviewed her for my first book, *In Her Own Voice: A Woman's*

Rise to CEO. To overcome these forces, Tonya believes in the power of showing men in leadership roles that they gain professionally when they help advance those who have been left out.

Women often are overlooked or devalued because of these "invisible forces" or ingrained assumptions or biases. When most people think of biased behavior, they think of a negative action taken deliberately. But implicit biases shape our behavior without us even realizing it. They are ever-present and powerful, and we all have them, no matter how well-intentioned we are. Human beings all carry the baggage of messages and lessons we have absorbed throughout our lives.[7] Even when we reject the idea that men are better suited to leadership than women, or that women are naturally superior caregivers than men, these concepts are still with us. Having an ingrained assumption doesn't make someone bad—it just means they're human.

Unlearning these biases is hard, and their traces can linger. But the good news is that it *is* possible to interrupt these deeply rooted assumptions, and the first step is awareness. Catalyst has created a suite of learning tools that help managers recognize the biases they may never have truly recognized for what they are.[8] I distinctly remember an exchange I had with one male manager after I had presented a talk at an event. He approached me to share that he thinks women make bad bosses, and he cited the example of a woman he worked for who was cutthroat and uncompromising and, at times, unkind.

After acknowledging how unfortunate that experience sounded, I asked him, "Have you worked for any men who behaved like that?"

"Yes, of course," he said.

"And would you say men are terrible to work for . . . or just that *those* men were bad bosses?"

I could practically see the light bulb go on over his head. "Oh," he said.

Oh, indeed.

This is an example both of attribution bias ("she was a bad boss *because* she was a woman, not just because she was a bad boss") and of confirmation bias ("I expect women to not be good managers, so when I find a bad woman manager, my beliefs are affirmed").[9] To interrupt these biases, we need to make the invisible visible. Once people become aware of these biases, they, too, can experience the light bulb moment that can lead to behavior change.

Dow Chair and CEO Jim Fitterling credits training about these invisible, ingrained assumptions for helping create an inclusive culture at his company. He told me, "We did [the training] in teams—product teams, business teams, manufacturing teams, and so on—across the globe. We walked through the different types of unconscious bias we might have, whether it's about race, gender, geography, and other viewpoints. People from different countries have different beliefs. And we found that a lot of people at Dow who went through this training took a step back and said, 'I didn't realize how strong some of my unconscious biases were until we did these exercises.' Having that awareness is always helpful."

To be clear, overt bias like Martin experienced continues to exist. But the type of bias most of us encounter in the workplace is of the implicit variety that Lynne faced—bias that can be challenging to see, even when it's right in front of us. Anyone perceived as not fitting the accepted vision of what a leader looks like is a potential victim.

After his "celebratory" dinner, Martin became hyperaware of all types of bias at work, whether overt or covert. He looked around at the women leaders at his company who "did not fit the dominant mold of people who were qualified and deserving of success. And what I saw was that they did not get the opportunities and promotions they should have." Martin also started scrutinizing the people with the power to grant opportunities and promotions, and he did not like what he saw. They were saying to themselves, and even out loud to colleagues, that certain roles required someone able to work hard, but then they'd dismiss certain hard workers by saying things like, "She's at an age where she's probably thinking about having a family," or "I'm not sure that person is a good cultural fit."

Martin continued, "All of these underlying assumptions and preconceived notions led to decisions made behind closed doors. And they were f–ing career killers."

These underlying assumptions and preconceived notions—the "invisible forces"—are especially pernicious. "When someone at work says something nasty about being gay, or being a woman of color, I hate to say this, but that's the least of our problems. It's the quiet, subtle, sharp things that professionals say behind closed doors that are really the things that inhibit career development and equality. That's the stuff that keeps me up at night," Martin said.

Look from a Different Perspective

David Simmonds, a Senior Vice President and Global Chief Communications and Sustainability Officer at Great-West Lifeco and Canada Life, is a true morning person and self-described "driver." By his 8:00 AM arrival at the office, he already has worked out and answered all his emails.

To David, his morning routine is just his personal preference. As a "failed varsity athlete," as he jokingly calls himself, he is accustomed to waking very early, but he didn't expect the same of others. He felt he had set the clear expectation for his team members, among whom are several parents with young children, that they could do whatever works for them. Most arrive at 9:00 AM.

One day his executive coach, Suzanne, offered him some feedback. She told him that many people on his team felt his words and actions were at odds; instead of encouraging each person to do what was best for their own schedule, they said he was sending a message that everyone needed to arrive as early as he did to be successful. They felt he didn't consider the fact that they had a lot of caregiving to do before they arrived at work, including dropping off their kids at school. David had never considered that he was transmitting this signal through his own behavior. In response, he followed the advice of his coach, who instructed him to arrive at 9:00 AM or later for eight weeks and see what happened.

"And so, I did that," David told me. "And I had a VP who came to me after about five weeks. She didn't know why my schedule had changed. She said, 'David, you would not believe the difference it's made for the rest of the team that you're walking in after we're already here.' It sounded simple, but changing my morning schedule even temporarily had a huge impact on me and my team. I realized that my role as a C-suite leader is not necessarily to do what I need to do to thrive. It's to do what my team needs. I needed to be more about empathy and understanding and giving people permission to do what they needed to do. And I am forever grateful to Suzanne for pointing this out to me."

7

Build Up What's in It for Men

5 B's of Gender Partnership

- ⊘ Begin with You
- ⊘ Break Down What's Not Working
- ⊘ **Build Up What's in It for Men**
- ○ Bridge the Gender Gaps
- ○ Bring Humanity to Work

Men stand to gain a lot from greater workforce fairness and inclusion. But historically, the benefits for men have not been a focal point of gender equity work, leaving many men feeling excluded and left behind. Gender partnership involves shining a light on the benefits for men so that they have a good reason and motivation to accept the invitation.

When men become gender partners in the workplace, their thinking shifts. They don't just become more aware of obstacles to fair and equal opportunities; they also become enthusiastic about partnering with women. In short, they move from the sidelines—apathy, ignorance, and fear (still keeping them from full engagement)—to awareness and then action.[1] To clarify, I don't mean "apathy" or "ignorance" in a derogatory way; these are the terms I used in chapter 3 to explain why men often don't realize they can have an impact, and, once they do understand and become committed to helping, they don't always know how to go about it.

One of the reasons men find themselves becoming enthusiastic about gender partnership is that they reap the rewards too. This aspect of the process just hasn't been as widely or openly discussed until now. The following sections discuss some key ways men benefit from gender equity in the workplace.

Men Enjoy Improved Work-Life Integration

Policies that enable women to balance career and other responsibilities, such as caring for children, are great for men too! According to the *New York Times*, many fathers took on more domestic work during the COVID stay-at-home orders of 2020 than they had previously. After the lockdown ended, a substantial share not only continued this practice but even rearranged their work lives to make more time for their families. A *New York Times* survey beginning in April 2020 and running through early 2023 showed that among heterosexual fathers, one-fifth continued to do more childcare than before the pandemic, and one-quarter continued to do more household work. "For these fathers," the *Times* said, "the pandemic offered a chance to reorganize their lives to be more involved in family life—and now, they don't want to give it up. Even before the pandemic, the generation of fathers currently raising children wanted to be more involved than their fathers had been, research has shown," but they encountered obstacles such as societal expectations about masculinity—obstacles that were overcome, at least in part, during the crisis of the pandemic.[2]

Inclusive workplace policies can also offer parents a path forward to ensure they have time with their families and households. Paul Hudson, CEO of Sanofi, is proud of his company's gender-neutral parental leave policy. He notes:

> Under this policy, men are just as likely as women to take 14 weeks off following the arrival of a new child. It has been a fantastic success, and it's a policy for everyone—for parents in same-sex relationships, for parents who adopted, for parents who had their child via surrogacy. What makes our policy beneficial *for women* is that a burden is lifted. When anyone can—and is expected to—take parental leave, then a woman doesn't have to worry about her commitment to work being questioned. If a man on her team is just as likely to take parental leave as she is, the playing field is leveled.

The benefit *for men* is that they, too, get to spend important bonding time with a new child without having to worry that their manager sees them as less masculine or insufficiently committed to their work. When all men eligible for parental leave take it, then the act of a man going on parental leave ceases to become a notable thing. It's just business as usual. This is what fairness looks like.

This type of equal opportunity must also be available throughout employees' life cycles, not just when there's a new baby on board. We all experience moments when we need to step away from our work during working hours—to take care of a sick family member, to attend a school event, or to be at home to meet the plumber when there's a leak. There doesn't need to be all this angst about being at home or taking a break to manage a crisis. "When I was younger, my wife and I both worked, and we had a newborn at the nursery," said Paul. "We would be texting each other constantly about which one of us could leave work and get to the nursery before it closed."

Paul notes that these moments, even when added up, represent just a small slice of an employee's time at work, yet "people feel them a lot. So I tell our leaders, and in particular our female leaders, that we're not clocking them in and out. All I really want to know is, at the end of the year, when you look back, did you work as the best version of yourself for the company? There's no need for people to judge themselves on a daily or weekly basis."

Unfortunately, many companies are not structured in a way that benefits women with families. For example, Paul observes that global companies offering international assignments "are set up for a man to be successful, [if he has] a woman or partner who follows him and looks after the kids. Very few global companies set up their international assignments for couples with dual careers, or with the woman being the one with the career."[3] This approach is ubiquitous but misguided. "If you're recruiting somebody who has talent, you need to make it easy for them to focus on what you're hiring them for. That means offering understanding and genuine empathy for what they're going through so that they feel safe to say, 'I just can't make this meeting, Paul.' It means showing that this is a long-term process, since 99 times out of 100 they're working hard and have earned that flexibility when they need it."

Amy Wilson, general counsel and corporate secretary for Dow, confirms that best-in-class family leave for everyone benefits men. Dow used to offer six weeks of maternity leave, but over the years, the company decided to create a more inclusive culture. Today, employees receive a global minimum standard of 16 weeks of paid parental leave, applying to all parents, birthing and non-birthing, whether through birth, adoption, or fostering.[4] "And everybody—junior-level, senior-level—feels comfortable taking that leave," Amy told me.

Those who don't need to take significant stretches of time off for personal reasons also benefit from small, daily moments of flexibility and integration, as Karl Preissner, Human Resources Director at P&G, notes. "The accountability and role-modeling of appropriate behaviors is important for all leaders, as these elements are crucial for moving toward an inclusive and gender-equal organization," he told me. "Support for parental leave policies is a key way our leaders demonstrate that employee development, both personal and professional, is more than just talk. When this commitment is clear, it shifts our culture, resulting in new behaviors. For example, more employees now feel comfortable sharing their personal experiences and connecting with colleagues outside of work."

For example, Karl's manufacturing colleagues report that informal conversations before the start of meetings have shifted from being entirely focused on sports to discussing topics such as children's dance festivals, volunteering at schools, and other personal interests. He's also seen a noticeable increase in discipline regarding the timely conclusion of afternoon meetings, allowing all employees to attend medical appointments, visit family members, or pick up children from extracurricular activities.

Through creating an inclusive culture that takes employees' full lives into account, companies create workplaces that work for women and also work for men.

Men Experience the Freedom That Comes from Breaking Out of the Man Box

When a male leader is vulnerable to his staff, he gives the men on his team a tremendous gift: permission to burst out of the restrictive man box. Even years later, employees remember the moment when the walls were broken down.

David Simmonds still talks about the day in 2019 when he worked at a health care company and he saw a talk by the company's new CEO. "He was giving a speech onstage about showing up and leaving it all on the field, even when you're not sure you can win. To drive home his point, he told a story about watching his son's youth football game. He pulled his arm back to show us how kids on the team were throwing the football. And as he did, he choked up. He talked about some of the worst passes being thrown—where these kids lacked for skill, there was no lack of effort. The team went out there on the field and did the work. As our new CEO was telling us this story, his emotion was palpable and powerful. The room applauded."

In those 30 seconds, everything changed. "There was permission to be honest," David explained to me. "This CEO set the tone for employees to feel free to openly discuss their fears about changes taking place within the company. I still have friends there, and it's an even stronger company today than it had been before. It's because the most senior leader at the company broke out of that box in front of all of us."

By putting his humanity on display in a moment of spontaneity, the CEO effectively showed employees they don't need to hide their emotions or vulnerability.

David, now Chief Marketing & Communications Officer at Canada Life & Great-West Lifeco, gives himself and others permission to bring "as much of themselves as they choose" to work. David shared, as an example, "the nail polish incident." It occurred during a video call that took place while he was spending the weekend in New York City during Pride festivities. Here's how he explains what happened:

I had all my friends at my apartment for the Pride March, but there was this acquisition I was working on, and I had to get on a video call. We were talking with the deal team on the way we wanted to frame the announcement. And I had forgotten that I'd painted my nails that day. One of my male colleagues on the call messaged me privately: "Is that purple on your fingernails?" And I messaged back: "No, it's aubergine." It was an interesting exchange because we had all these big companies on the call, and I was really serious about the deal, and I talk with my hands. And my nails were this shimmering shade of purple!

People in the company talk about it. I basically gave a whole bunch of people permission to just be themselves because they've seen, or heard about, a senior-level guy wearing nail polish on an important call.

What makes the nail polish story, as well as the football story, so powerful is that these were unplanned moments. They happened organically and were authentic. Neither David nor the new CEO woke up that morning thinking, *Today, I am going to bring my full self to work!* You shouldn't have to apologize for who you are. Feeling comfortable with yourself enables others to feel that they, too, can express themselves openly, and that can lead them to feel more invested in the company and willing to share more innovative and courageous ideas.

Men Reap the Benefits of a Workplace Culture Where Everyone Feels Safe

Dow Chair and CEO Jim Fitterling is committed to creating a workplace in which employees would want their family members to work. "One thing I always ask people is, 'Would you want your son or daughter, or your next-door-neighbor's kids, to work here?' Which is another way of saying, 'What kind of place do you want this to be?' If someone you care about said they wanted to work here, would you feel proud—or scared?" The foundation of creating a company where people want to work is safety—both psychological and physical. This book is mostly focused on the mental and emotional well-being of employees, but the other side of that coin is that physical safety matters too. For example, employees will be more likely to speak up when they witness a safety violation if they know they won't be punished for naming the problem, even if it means contradicting senior leadership.[5] "We work with products that require safe handling," Jim told me, "and we work with big equipment and machinery. There are always risks in the workplace. So we need this to be a physically safe place. But in order to make it physically safe, it also has to be psychologically safe. In an environment like this, you need to look out for your own safety, but we really want you to also look out for your team members, to think about other people, not just yourself."

"Safety" can mean different things to women than it does to men, so creating a safe workplace necessarily involves being aware of issues specific to gender and being willing to make changes so that everyone feels protected.[6] "You've got to understand the threats out there for women that may not be the same as for men," Jim continued. "If somebody's working late at night, and they have to get their car in the dark, and they're alone, then hey, someone needs to make sure it's safe for them. We talk about situations like this at safety meetings to ensure that no one is being put at risk."

And Dow brings the same commitment to ensuring psychological safety since both forms of safety are foundational to inclusion. It's not just about physical plant conditions; it's about how people communicate with each other. "You want to make sure that if [an employee is] in a commercial negotiation that they're not taken advantage of. You need to train people to have awareness and not assume that everyone experiences things the same way."

Training leaders and employees to look out for each other benefits everyone. It also strengthens the quality of work. Innovation best occurs in the absence of fear and within an environment where people have the ability to speak their mind. Psychological safety, in short, is good for business. When everyone has trust that they can speak up without facing repercussions, morale improves, and both the employees and the organization are better positioned for high performance.[7]

Men Gain New Skills and Experience Personal Satisfaction Through Gender Partnership

If you had asked my husband, Chip McCollum, in the past about advancing women, he might have said, "I understand why you think it's important, but it's not really my role." Then he had an experience that changed him.

He was working as a banker in sales for a large financial services company when he saw that a colleague, a young woman named Irina who was great at her job, had endless potential but was not getting promoted. I told Chip, "Given your experience, you're in the perfect position to help her succeed!" And I recall him saying, "I'm an individual contributor. I don't manage a team. I'm not an executive. There's really nothing I can do." I gently disagreed and asked whether he had expertise and real-world experience getting promoted himself. I shared that I believed he could easily mentor and coach her because he had already achieved what she wanted. This is where I saw him shift from apathy to action—a move that benefited not only Irina but himself.

Here is the story, in Chip's own words:

When I met Irina, she was working for a vice president who had some shortfalls. I first noticed her potential during a meeting about a deal we were trying to get approved. Some critical questions had been raised, and her boss didn't know the answers. I could tell by Irina's responses that she was perfectly capable of figuring out what we needed to know.

We decided to stop the meeting because we weren't getting the information we needed from Irina's boss [the vice president]. I went to Irina's cubicle, and we looked at the computer together. I helped her determine which financial statements to pull, which numbers to source, and how to package it up. In talking with Irina, I realized she was brilliant. I also saw right away she wasn't getting this kind of training from her boss. She said, "I can't believe this . . . you're so helpful. I really appreciate you taking the time."

To make sure she got credit for the work, I later circled back and told the team leader who oversaw the whole department—Irina's boss's boss—that she was the brains behind it. He said, "We know that. We want her to be more confident and speak up more." That gave me the context to help her with that specific goal in mind.

A few months later, I went to Irina and said, "I think there's a problem with our internal pricing model." She said, "Yes, I'm seeing that too." She showed some calculations, and it confirmed what I thought.

I said, "I think you could run the math to identify the problem in the model and then create a presentation." I suggested she take it to the head of corporate finance, and we agreed on the message she would deliver: "We've got a problem here; our model is not calculating our returns properly and when it's compared to other groups within the company, we're coming out lower." So, with my encouragement, she met with the head of the group. That put a massive star on her forehead from that point on.

This is a great example of sponsorship in action. Chip had started by mentoring Irina, then moved to coaching her, and then to sponsoring her by going to her department head to surface her excellence. Chip endorsed her by using his own influence and credibility for her benefit: "You've got to watch her. She's the one with the talent."

By the time Chip left the company to accept a new position at another bank, Irina was well on her way up. One day, she reached out to him and invited him to lunch. Chip remembers:

> When I was leaving my old bank, I had suggested Irina come with me to the new one. We could have used her talent. So, when she reached out to me, I had hoped she was going to take me up on the offer. During lunch she told me she had an exceptional opportunity internally, but it was a difficult negotiation. They wanted to move her to a different group and give her more responsibility but leave her with an associate title, making it a lateral move.
>
> In our industry, titles are a big deal: They put you on a different rung on the ladder for base pay and bonuses. In her current position, she was on the doorstep of becoming a vice president, which is a great title because it means you can lead deal teams. If she took the new job, she would have to start over again and work her way back up.
>
> My advice was, "No, they want you. Buckle down and tell them you want the VP title, and you want the raise, and you're not coming otherwise." I helped her see she had leverage she hadn't even been aware of, and I tried to build her confidence in asking for what she deserved.
>
> Irina was nervous about the thought of having to go to the opposite side of the table with her new boss. But she did, and it ended up being a weeklong negotiation. Then she called me and said, "I've got some news for you." So, we went to lunch again and she told me, "I got the promotion, I got the title, I got the raise." Along the way I've helped guys in this way, too, but I find they don't often need additional coaching and

encouragement—not necessarily because men are better at their jobs but because people in leadership positions tend not to need a nudge to promote men the way they often do for women. It's generally accepted that if a guy is good at his job and doing deals, he's going to get promoted. This is not necessarily the case with women. They have to advocate for themselves and make the ask, which they're often reluctant to do. They tend to take what the organization gives them, and then if they don't feel good about it, they may leave. That's a lose-lose situation. But if you encourage them and help them formulate an argument and help them build their confidence, it becomes a win-win.

Today, Chip works as a managing director for another large global bank. He learned so much from his experience helping Irina advance that he seeks out opportunities to do something similar at his current job:

The more deals you work on, the more experienced you become. You can't create that overnight. You must have that experience to go out in the world and sell the firm's products and services. If you put someone in that role just to check a box—man or woman—you set them up for failure.

But not as many women in our field have this background, so here's what my team is doing. There are six salespeople in my group, all white men in our upper forties and fifties. We know that's got to change. We've created an associate relationship manager role to work alongside us, to give them a front-row seat on the customer-facing teams. There are two of them, both young women in their late twenties, and they're rising stars. They're gaining deal knowledge, building intellectual capital, and learning how to become effective relationship managers.

They're getting a view into this world that they couldn't get in many other places.

Darci is my associate relationship manager. I bring her to as many meetings as I can, and I ask her to create our work product to send out on our behalf. It's not me repackaging her work; I want her to get the credit.

One time at a meeting I introduced myself, talked about our group, and said, "Darci works on our team." When it was her turn to speak, she said, "I support Chip." I talked to her afterward and advised, "Don't say that. Instead, say that you're on the originations team and we work on deals together." I don't want her to be perceived as an assistant.

Ensuring she is successful requires giving her stretch experiences. I want Darci to build intellectual capital and learn how to do things on her own. I want her to see that every case is different, which gives her a broader mindset. She will then be able to not only create the work product but think critically about it.

Advocating for Irina and Darci has been incredibly rewarding for Chip. He has learned what it looks like to be a coach, a mentor, and a sponsor. He feels good helping others live up to their potential. And now he actively seeks out opportunities to advocate for women, even if they are not his direct colleagues.

As Chip notes, sometimes these opportunities present themselves organically.

Bela has been working for a real estate investment company for more than five years. I met her in person for the first time at a client dinner in New York. The guests were mostly investors—almost all men—and Bela was the highest-ranking investor relations person in the room. To give some perspective, she is one of only a few female client-facing employees of this firm.

The rest are male, including two other members of the investor relations team who report to her.

When I walked in, I noticed she was in the corner writing out name tags. Her two direct reports were walking around shaking hands and greeting the guests. I approached her and said, "Why are you doing the name tags?" She said, "Oh, it's just easier. I have better handwriting, and I know who's coming. I invited them."

That wasn't really adding up for me, but I let it go. When the event started, the CEO had everyone around the room introduce themselves and ask an initial question to drive the conversation. He needed somebody from his team to capture the questions so he could make sure he answered them all. Well, Bela was sitting there with a piece of paper and pen, and the two other investor relations guys weren't. So, as the CEO opened the meeting, he looked over and saw Bela writing. He said, "Bela, are you getting all this?" She said yes.

Remember: The predominant gender in the room was male. And here's Bela, the lone woman in the room and on her team, anointed the scribe for the dinner. Afterward, I decided to say something. "Bela, this is not your role. You brought all these people together. You're a host, not an administrator. You've got two people that work for you. They need to be making name tags. They need to make sure there are enough chairs. They need to be writing down questions—not you. You're the money raiser."

She said, "Wow, you know, I never really thought about that. I just tend to jump in and do things. I want to be helpful."

I said, "I know you're helping, but you need to delegate and let your team be helpful too. Doing these more administrative tasks keeps you from connecting with clients and handling the more important things that are aligned with what you're responsible for."

It was like a light bulb went on in her head. Since then, I have noticed she is very aware of staying in her senior role, and it shows up in other areas of her work. For instance, I called her recently and said, "We want to invest in a specific property in Austin." She said, "That's great. I'll have Dylan contact you, and he will get all the information."

Chip's role in sponsoring Irina in her company set him up to mentor Darci and also to coach Bela. In the past, he might not have noticed what was happening at the investment dinner (and if he had, he would probably have thought, *It isn't my job to get involved*). But now, because of his previous results, he looks for occasions to step up.

That is what gender partnership looks like. When men start advocating for women, it also fills their cup. The successes inspire them, propel them forward, and make them want to do more. The research backs it up: Men who engage as gender partners report psychological and social benefits.[8]

I love these stories not only because several high-achieving women are now positioned for even greater heights, but because the narratives also demonstrate how personally fulfilling gender partnership can be. Chip sums it up best: "Not only have I enhanced my own leadership skills; I've also widened my network and even my ability to see what's going on in a room. I'm definitely sharper now. Plus, these experiences have made me a better person."

8

Bridge the Gender Gaps

5 B's of Gender Partnership

- ⊘ Begin with You
- ⊘ Break Down What's Not Working
- ⊘ Build Up What's in It for Men
- ⊘ **Bridge the Gender Gaps**
- ○ Bring Humanity to Work

Gaps persist between women and men in pay, leadership representation, and intangibles such as recognition, safety, and engagement. Gender partners can bridge these gaps by helping to identify and remove the barriers that prevent all talent from benefiting from fair systems and inclusive cultures.

You've learned about how to **Begin** gender partnership by self-reflecting and using your personal influence, to **Break Down** societal expectations about women and men, and **Build Up** for men what they gain through an inclusive work culture. Now, it's time to **Bridge** the opportunity and fairness gaps that keep women from achieving pay equity and career development and advancement. Through the experiences of corporate leaders, let's explore Catalyst's guidance to create an inclusive and fair workplace where no one is left behind.

Expand the Table: Include More Diversity at the Executive Level

We already know that businesses are healthier when their leadership is gender balanced. But removing barriers from the system to enable equity of opportunity—and waiting for it to pay dividends in talent outcomes—takes time. Yet this is the approach Catalyst and the companies that support us know is essential for driving meaningful and sustainable business impact. So what should executives do when they have the need but not the time to ensure the voices around the table reflect their total talent pool and the clients and communities they serve? Two things. First, take the strategic road in fixing any systemic barriers; this is the right road for the long term. But *also* take intentional action now. For example, if there are limited place settings at your leadership table and you think the only way to make space for women is to remove men—qualified men whose leadership remains critical—think again. If you don't want to miss out on perspectives of a broader set of qualified talent, the answer is simple: Get a bigger table.

This is what Christian, the European global pharma executive, has done many times in his career. He knows that diverse teams with a good gender mix create better solutions,[1] so he expands the number of people on his leadership team, a move that allows him to add different capabilities and perspectives and to make it more diverse and inclusive. "I also include the next level of leaders in the organization by forming an extended leadership team with my direct reports and select people who are important multipliers in the organization. Currently, this is a team of around 80 people. I made the circle bigger not only for women but for change agents across the organization from different functions and regions."

He added, "There is power in having a good gender mix, and people with very different backgrounds. This allows for better decision-making and better solutions to create much more value."

Christian continued:

In most businesses I've led, when I started, there was limited diversity on the leadership team. I've always tried to build teams that are more diverse, that bring in different perspectives. When you have diverse teams, you actually create a totally different culture in the entire organization. More ideas are brought to life. I think with an environment where you allow for a full array of opinions, it changes the way you serve customers; it changes the way you collaborate with business partners; and it changes the way you innovate.

But the composition of the team does not, all by itself, lead to better business outcomes. Diverse teams must be coupled with an inclusive leadership style[2]—and gender partners like Christian are very intentional in the way they lead. He told me, "I want to be the most collaborative person you will find, and I want to build the most collaborative team you will find."

To ensure the table always has this mix, he says, "you create certain simple rules around the hiring process in your organization. I have set the expectation that every interview panel has to ideally include male and female interviewers, and in every final set of candidates, we need to aspire to have male and female candidates to interview." Every organization will tackle these approaches differently depending on their regional context, organizational strategy, and specific goals. But generally these are the sorts of talent strategies that enable organizations to move away from quotas and avoid complacency around the status quo. They instead bake fairness checks into the system that allow barriers to be removed and help the best, most qualified talent, from any background, to be seen and supported.

Christian has found throughout his career that having a gender-balanced and diverse work environment translates to better business results.

Elevate Each Other

At Catalyst we often explain the distinction between mentorship and sponsorship by noting that a mentor talks *with* an employee while a sponsor talks *about* the employee.[3] This principle applies outside of formal sponsorship too. To be seen and to advance, it's essential to have advocates who help elevate your achievements.

Women face an obstacle that men do not: We are expected to be likable. As I shared in chapter 1, I was perceived as unlikable early in my career when I worked on the Atlanta Olympic Games. The root cause for this perception was the dominant belief that women should be soft and agreeable, which goes hand in hand with a bias against women who are tough and determined. Likewise, gender bias dictates that women should refrain from promoting themselves, and that doing so is unseemly and "unladylike."

But we all know that self-promotion is essential to getting ahead. If we don't tout our achievements, we risk being overlooked. So what are women supposed to do? Executive leadership coach and author Mark Thompson relies on a genius hack for women to circumvent gender bias. It is called "collaborative promotion."

Here's the secret: Instead of calling out your own achievements, buddy up with someone and then *each of you calls out the other person's achievements*.

"We call out somebody else and promote what they're great at," Mark explained to me. "So I'll say, 'Jennifer's one of the best CEOs I've ever met, for these three reasons.' And then you will say, 'And Mark's a great coach, who has helped me personally.' It has to be done in a sincere way. Everybody listening trusts both of us more now. We are both lifted up. This collaborative promotion works much better than if you were to tout yourself and I were to tout myself. And this is especially true for women, because the research shows that people are still quite harsh about women talking about themselves as being the best at what they do. So collaborative promotion ends up being a powerful hack."

I agree with Mark that it's a proven tactic that helps colleagues, especially women, who are judged harshly when they lift themselves up. I would add that this tactic requires intentional effort, repeated over time, so that we develop "muscle memory" and the act of promoting other people becomes natural. I have used it myself many times as part of the 100 Coaches Community, which was founded by Marshall Goldsmith and where I met Mark. The 100 Coaches is a group of coaches, consultants, authors, and CEOs, all aligned around a common purpose to elevate the impact of world-class leadership professionals through connection and learning. They are among the most exceptional people I have ever met, and we are committed to lifting each other up so we can have greater success and impact individually and collectively. We comment and post positively on each other's LinkedIn profiles; we promote each other's books and accomplishments; we speak at each other's events; and we broker introductions to further our respective aspirations.

Sarah McArthur, editor-in-chief of the journal *Leader to Leader*, is another extraordinary collaborative promoter. She helped further shape Alan Mulally's "Working Together" system, his leadership and management approach focused on collaboration and shared purpose.

Sarah also worked jointly with Marshall and the legendary business-woman and Girl Scouts CEO Frances Hesselbein on the book *Work Is Love Made Visible* (for which Alan wrote the foreword), about the importance of leaders creating collaborative cultures. All four leaders intentionally have elevated others. Sarah describes the ethos of the 100 Coaches Community as "knocking on doors, opening them, and bringing other people through the doors with them." Mark observes that some people worry that if they elevate someone else, it will become zero-sum, and that by lifting up another person they implicitly lower themselves. Nonsense, he says. "The person who's doing the promotion to the other gets a lift, and so does the person receiving it."

Mark was inspired to employ this partnership tool by his wife, Bonita Thompson, a leadership expert and author. In her PhD dissertation, "How Leaders Develop Collaborative Leadership for Effectiveness,"[4] she demonstrates the significance of relationship-building for effective leadership. Her thesis is that organizations promote people based on their abilities to stand out from the crowd with confidence, assertiveness, and dominance. Yet, once promoted into a leadership role, their effectiveness is judged on their ability to accomplish their goals through others. "These are very different skill sets," Bonita explained to me. "My research looked at how leaders learn the collaborative skills that frame leadership effectiveness. It doesn't specifically focus on gender. To my knowledge, there are no assessment tools available to make the claim that women are better at these skills."

Yet we have seen that many people harbor a bias (which they may not consciously be aware of) against women leaders because they perceive them as valuing relationships too much and at the expense of good decision-making. Bonita's research of board members, CEOs, C-suite leaders, and mid-level managers working in for-profit US companies is paradigm-shifting because it proves that to be successful you must have relationship-building skills; 91% reported that collaboration with people who don't report to them was an essential part of their job.

Put another way: Organizations that overlook women, intentionally or not, because of gender bias are hurting their business because they are excluding a lot of talent with needed skills.

Include Those Left Out: Find Them and Invite Them

As Kenji Yoshino of the Meltzer Center for Diversity, Inclusion, and Belonging often says, "Talent is everywhere, opportunity is not." At Catalyst, we could not agree more. But we also know that business leaders often struggle to build a robust pipeline of qualified talent across a range of backgrounds.[5] One concern I hear a lot is, "I would love to promote women—but there aren't enough talented and qualified women in the pipeline!" But how can that be? The reality is that there are plenty of talented and qualified women in your field—no matter what industry you work in. You just need to make an effort to actively find them and make them part of your pipeline. Talent is everywhere; it just may not be sitting on your doorstep. This is why at Catalyst we tell leaders to look broad, look deep, and look often.

Gerald Lema—a Tokyo-based partner at the global venture capital company Reaction; chairman and managing partner of the private investment group Windward Capital Ventures; and a member of the Catalyst Board of Directors—has lived in different regions around the globe, from Australia to Germany, Hong Kong, and Turkey. A number of years ago, while in Japan as Chairman of Baxter International Japan, he noticed that the women in the organization were not returning to work after their maternity leave—and after being out of the labor force for several years, they found it challenging to reenter once their children went to school. Yet they were educated star performers and highly sought-after employees. His company was being dealt a blow by their departure. He wanted their talent back.

Gerald's team did some sleuthing and discovered that many mothers gathered, with their children in tow, at Tokyo cafés to network and socialize. Gerald sent his assistant, herself a mother, to go and chat with them. "She asked, 'Have you worked in finance? Do you want to come in and talk with us?' In Japan, it's mandatory to send your children to kindergarten, so we knew that the women might be interested in reentering the workforce at that time. And we were able to hire many amazing women this way."

Gerald was a highly effective gender partner: He saw that mothers needed an on-ramp back to the workforce, so he went out of his way to find them, create the ramp, and guide them to it. His plan involved ingenuity, creative thinking, and determination, and the outcome was a win for everyone.

Mark and Gerald, in different ways, observed that women were being left out, and developed a plan to reverse course. What they have done is good for women and good for business.

Employee resource groups (ERGs), or affinity groups, can also serve this role of identifying and lifting up qualified but overlooked talent.[6] While everyone should be invited to ERGs, they provide a space for employees with similar identities or interests to connect with one another, which helps with engagement and retention. Dow's ERGs are open to everyone—those who are members of the identity group as well as their allies. Their first ERG was the Women's Inclusion Network, which was soon joined by nine other groups, including the Asian Diversity Network, the Disability Employee Network, the Global African Affinity Network, and GLAD (the chemical industry's first affinity group for LGBTQ+ employees). One of the groups is for employees over 50, another is for new employees, and together they represent a powerful community of cross-generational talent. Over 60% of Dow employees are part of one or more networks.

As Jim Fitterling ticked off the names of Dow's 10 employee resource groups (ERGs), it was evident to me that he felt a sense of pride about building a workplace that not only aimed to be inclusive but that encouraged these groups to act with trust and transparency in their interactions with the company. Members of Dow's ERGs assess and problem-solve workplace issues, which they are encouraged to bring to senior leadership. "These groups tackle some of the unwritten rules, some of the issues that their population may be dealing with, and they do it in a space with allies to raise awareness. They have a voice to bring up these issues to management, and we act on what they tell us. And we have no double standards; the way I treat somebody in the plant is no different from the way I treat someone on the executive management team."

This is one of the reasons that Dow has received certification from Great Place to Work, and *Fortune* named Dow as one of the top 25 World's Best Workplaces™.[7] Jim says, "We've got business that we have to do, but we're also a family unit, and we make sure we're looking after everybody." By inviting everyone to connect with one another, Dow builds a workplace culture of inclusion.

Model Accountability: Give Credit and Amplify the Contributions of Others

One of the metaphors we often invoke at Catalyst is that of the pebble in the pond. It's the idea that a small action can have significant ripple effects. During one of our MARC workshops, a participant named Sean remembered that a woman colleague, Anita, asked to meet with him after an executive meeting they were both in.[8] She said, "I am not sure you are aware of this, but you took credit for an idea I had during the meeting." He asked her to explain, and she described how he had repeated her idea and then everyone else in the room had immediately given him credit. He felt embarrassed and confused; it had not been his intention to take credit. He thanked her for making him aware and agreed that in the future if he does repeat something he hears, he will first state the name of the person who said it.

At the next meeting, he tried this out and was surprised by the results. Not only did he notice the appropriate people getting credit, but he also became keenly aware how often this happened to women in other meetings with men. After spending some time reflecting on this phenomenon, he realized that the issue was both that he had been given credit and that Anita had not. Meaning, it wasn't just a matter of him getting credit when he repeated the idea, but why had Anita's contribution not been acknowledged in the first place?

Sean now understood that he had a responsibility not only to avoid getting credit for a woman's idea but also to proactively ensure he used his voice to amplify the ideas of women. This realization allowed him to also pay it forward, as working on his own behavior change also made him better able to help other men become aware of this dynamic and learn how to be better gender partners.

Sean's behavior is a beautiful example of two employees working on mutual accountability. Anita spoke up to Sean without shaming or blaming him about behavior that shut her out from the recognition she deserved and needed to succeed in their workplace. Sean owned his behavior, reflected on it with humility, took action to correct it, and shared his learning with other men to ensure that others would not repeat his error.

Create an Atmosphere of Safety: Don't Shame People Who Make Honest Mistakes

In Catalyst research on what makes a strong, inclusive leader, one of the behaviors that rises to the top is humility. Specifically, displaying humility involves taking ownership for mistakes and learning from missteps. When a leader not only embodies this behavior but encourages it, they build within employees trust, a sense of feeling valued, the latitude to make mistakes without being penalized, and the security to take risks, and the result will be positive. Inclusive leadership behaviors like humility drive employee experiences of inclusion, which then drive outcomes like innovation and engagement.[9] None of this can happen in an environment of competition, shame, and retribution.

Jim Fitterling, Chair and CEO of Dow, lives by the golden rule of treating others at least as well as he wants to be treated, if not better. And he discusses this leadership approach regularly. As a result, the culture at Dow emphasizes constructive, positive criticism—which is more likely to occur when leaders are humble, take accountability for their errors, and don't assume they're always right. "We don't tear people down or attack," Jim tells me. "And I say that because there was a time in history where I think it was fairly common in corporate America that one of the ways to get ahead was by making the other guy look bad." But here is where the mutual accountability piece comes in. Jim not only ensures that Dow rejects combativeness; he also makes sure to "be the keeper" of the new workplace norms. "You've got to make sure that the workplace doesn't become toxic, that it stays positive."

When I met with Jim's colleague Amy Wilson, general counsel and corporate secretary, she confirmed that, at Dow, when someone makes a mistake, no one points fingers. Instead, everyone comes together to solve the problem. She told us a story about a junior colleague who, several years ago, accidentally sent a draft earnings release with a cost-cutting announcement to a financial media editor a few days before it was due to be released. The head of communications showed up in Amy's office and said, "You won't believe what just happened." Amy says a Dow representative called the reporter and explained that the announcement had been sent in error, but the reporter said they were going to run the story within the hour.

As I listened to Amy, I couldn't stand the suspense. Talk about a corporate nightmare!

Amy continued, "The leadership team huddled in the conference room and discussed what to do, since we hadn't planned to make the announcement until after the board meeting two days later, and now we had less than an hour to prepare. And we just pulled everything together. Not once in that process did somebody say, 'Who did this, and when are we going to take their head off?' Instead, the attitude in the room was: 'Okay, this mistake happened, now what are we going to do about it?' We saved the postmortem for another day."

I didn't ask Amy if the person who made the mistake was a woman, because it didn't matter. The point is that everyone, regardless of gender, and especially those who may be more junior, benefits when the workplace culture emphasizes collaborative problem-solving, not finger-pointing. In this environment, people have the psychological safety to make mistakes.[10]

A culture of psychological safety—where employees feel comfortable not only taking risks and making mistakes but also expressing opinions that might not be widely shared—is necessary for gender partnership to flourish.[11] We know that employees, especially women, may be afraid to take risks at work because they fear being punished, perhaps disproportionately compared to male colleagues, if they make mistakes.[12] But you need to take risks to ascend to leadership roles. A workplace where everyone knows they can confide in their manager and confess their errors is one that works for women and for everyone.

After all, whose doorway do people want to show up in when there's a problem? Do they want to show up in the one belonging to the screamer, the person who yells, "How could this have happened?!"

Or do they want to show up in the doorway of the person who says, "Okay, we're going to talk later about how this mistake happened, but right now we're going to talk about what we do about it. And I'm glad you told me. I'm glad you felt *comfortable* telling me. Where do we go from here?"

Jim adds, "Leaders must think about psychological safety in the same way they think about physical safety. In fact, the two are very much related. As leaders, it's our job to create a culture where people feel motivated and empowered to help course-correct when the situation calls for it. To create the right culture and environment, you must also be mindful of what challenges your people are facing—and that gets very personal. But you need to have trust and a good relationship with your team to have those discussions. Caring is part of building that trust, plus the actions you take to make a difference. It's up to us as leaders to create an environment where our teams feel valued and understood so they can safely speak up and help us do even better."[13]

CHEVRON'S BLUEPRINT

What does gender partnership look like at the organizational level? Chevron provides an excellent case study of best practices.

After learning about MARC in 2016, Chevron CEO Mike Wirth realized that bringing the program to Chevron would be a fantastic benefit to the organization, since the only training on gender equity was taking place at the executive level. As executive sponsor of Chevron's Women's Employee Network (WEN), Mike asked WEN's leaders to design and launch a MARC program. Under the supervision of Senior Earth Scientist Kat Hoffman, Chevron was the first Catalyst supporter to launch a pilot program.

Here is what Kat told us:

Within two years of the pilot kickoff, which was a tremendous success (150 people attended the kickoff, nearly doubling our goal of 80 people), Chevron had launched a MARC program (the self-led, small group discussion–based MARC Dialogue Teams) on every continent on which it operates. Both men and women employees continue to be active participants. In the years since, MARC has flourished within Chevron, and gender equity has become a central part of our organizational culture. While there is still work to do, we are proud of all we have accomplished.

Here are the principles and tactics we have used (and continue to use) in creating and supporting our change initiative. At Chevron, we hope that other organizations can use these practices as a blueprint to create a best-odds approach to supporting gender equity in their own cultures.

Design a Culture-Change Initiative

Make sure culture change starts at the top. Although grassroots movements can (and often do) gain traction, Mike Wirth and other leaders knew it was important for this type of culture change to start at the top. Our gender equity movement would have the best odds for success if leaders were publicly on board from the beginning. When leaders unite *with* employees around a common opportunity, employees feel seen and heard. Culture change becomes mainstream and gains momentum.

Then, push change initiatives toward the front lines. Too often, employees may not see leaders' decisions and actions, and, as a result, change initiatives stay clustered toward the top. We wanted gender equity to permeate our organization, so our leaders committed to pushing training and development throughout Chevron's hierarchy.

Use the Win, Build, Send model. We designed our MARC program based on the "Win, Build, Send" model:

- **Win** people over.
- **Build** up their skill set.
- **Send** employees out to put those skills to use, talk about the program, and begin winning new participants over.

Win People Over

Partner with existing evangelists first. (They are the lowest-hanging fruit!) We were very thoughtful about how we could encourage men to sign up for MARC. Instead of requiring an entire department or team to do MARC training, we kicked off our initiative by partnering with male leaders like Mike Wirth who were already gender equity allies and advocates. Some of these men agreed to be leaders in the program; others committed to attend and participate in meetings.

Use the buddy system. Encourage interested employees to invite their peers. Many of the male allies we recruited sent their male colleagues personal invitations to attend the pilot kickoff event, which was key to getting men to sign up and stick with the program. We also encouraged women to attend the pilot kickoff.

Make the program predictable. For newcomers to commit to a program like MARC, they need to know what to expect. Reducing variance helps, including regular meeting frequency, time, and place.

Share data to sway skeptics. We collected foundational data, which was crucial in getting skeptics on board. It's hard to argue with numbers, which can often override loudly voiced opinions or widespread misconceptions. Numbers can convince people that there *is* an issue that needs to be addressed via culture change.

Highlight why employees should care. Employees should know why culture change will benefit the company, but it's also important for them to understand how the initiative might impact them personally. We focused on the fact that gender equity benefits everyone, not just women.

Expect some initial resistance—but don't let it stop you. At first, many women were skeptical of what they saw as men trying to "fix" the gender equity issue. In MARC's early days, we frequently got asked why men were part of the explicit focus of the program. Continue reading to learn how we addressed this type of resistance.

Build Employees' Skill Sets

Give your program a long runway. Chevron's MARC pilot lasted one year, with groups meeting monthly. We knew that if MARC only spanned a few meetings, it ran the risk of being a "check the box" initiative instead of a sustained push toward lasting change. It takes time to break down assumptions and biases, and to establish the psychological safety people need to self-reflect, admit where they have been wrong, and evolve.

Build trust in small groups. When there are fewer people in the room, employees will be more honest, open, and vulnerable. They can get to know each other better, which means that later they may feel comfortable asking one another for support and advice.

Include a leader in each group. We found that it was especially powerful to include a higher-level leader in each small group. This demonstrated that Chevron was fully invested in the MARC program. It also helped employees feel heard by their leaders, which helped build trust across the power gradient. In turn, leaders were able to efficiently escalate frontline suggestions up the organizational hierarchy.

As a side note, placing a leader in each small group was a powerful incentive for some employees to join and commit to MARC. Having the opportunity to regularly meet with a leader who might be multiple levels up the organizational hierarchy is not an opportunity many people get.

Create a common language that everyone can use. We encouraged MARC leaders to use the language of gender equity going forward, so they could communicate consistently what was happening within the company and why. Sometimes organizations take important action, but employees don't realize what is happening because no one has told them; using terms and phrases people were familiar with from the MARC program helped bridge that gap.

Provide topics for conversation. Better yet, create a company-wide discussion calendar. Culture change is driven by open, honest dialogue. Chevron's Women's Employee Network sent out a monthly letter to MARC groups identifying topics for discussion. (This letter was also a good opportunity to introduce and reinforce common language.) Early discussion topics were lower stakes; as time went on and groups built trust, they tackled thornier issues.

Emphasize individual progress. Culture change throughout an organization begins with individual employees who look inward and commit to growth. While we met regularly in groups, we also put a lot of emphasis on individual progress. This work almost always began with helping employees discover their own unconscious biases, examine why those biases exist, and take action to change their behaviors.

One woman expressed a sentiment we've heard from other women in the MARC program: "I joined this program thinking it would be about telling men how they needed to change. But I've realized I have a lot of unconscious biases too. Men face barriers and fears that I wasn't aware of. I need to work on being a better advocate for men!"

Build awareness by discussing headwinds and barriers. It's important that employees have the opportunity to listen to others and (hopefully) discover some of their own implicit biases. We found that, for a variety of reasons, men often don't realize the challenges and barriers women face in the workplace. Mike Wirth shared that his first three supervisors at Chevron were women, so he didn't "see" the problem; in other words, he didn't realize that women might not have the same career opportunities that men may have. He later realized that these women were the exception, not the rule.

Use internal surveys and share statistics. As mentioned earlier, data is a powerful tool when it comes to educating employees (including revealing biases and exposing misconceptions). Chevron conducted several anonymous surveys about our organization's culture that were eye-opening for men. The resulting data demonstrated clearly that gender inequity was a problem in *our* organization, not "something that happens in other companies." We shared the content of surveys, as well as their results, in monthly letters to MARC groups, which sparked further discussion in meetings.

Send Employees Out

Educate employees on specific actions to take and words to use. Shifting people's beliefs and assumptions—which is what happens in the Win and Build stages—is a necessary first step in a change initiative. But pervasive, systemic change won't happen unless employees' behaviors and actions also change. Therein lies the problem: People often want to do the right thing but simply don't know how.

That's why we gave our MARC groups tangible examples of things they could say and do to advance gender equity. We knew that when employees had the right language and tools, they would be more likely to act. We focused on providing specific tactics for specific problems. For example, if a man sees a woman being overlooked in a meeting, what can he do to highlight her contributions and bring her into the discussion?

We ultimately found that men who participated in MARC were two times as likely to speak up if they saw exclusionary behaviors—and women were three and a half times more likely. Men reported that they'd previously stayed silent because they were wary of saying the wrong thing. Having a script to use gave them the confidence to step up. Women said that the script also empowered them to speak up in a way that wouldn't be viewed as "complaining."

Give groups assignments to make the work real and relevant between meetings. It's difficult for culture change to take root if employees only think about it once a month at a meeting. We encouraged MARC members to read, learn, discuss, and apply concepts between meetings via informal "homework" assignments.

Eventually, hand the baton to men. They are in the best position to drive progress. Once the MARC program was up and running, I purposefully took a step back so that others could step up. Specifically, I wanted men to be in charge. I knew that they would be able to make changes I might not have thought of, and I didn't want them to feel like they had to run their ideas past me. Men have led MARC at Chevron since 2019.

Ongoing Best Practices

We know that gender equity at Chevron won't be achieved through a one-and-done program, so we continue to invest in culture change. Now that our pilot program has concluded, Win, Build, and Send are continuously occurring in various MARC groups. We've found that the following best practices help keep our program agile as it moves forward and evolves.

Look for signs that culture change is growing organically. When we see employees organically acting in ways that advance gender fairness or demonstrate allyship, it tells us that our initiative is taking root in Chevron's culture. This qualitative evidence is just as important as gathering quantitative data because it lets us know that our initiative is on track (or, conversely, that we might need to change course).

One early sign that Chevron's culture was changing was seeing things like "Dads and Donuts" or "School pick-up" on men's public calendars. Before the MARC program, these things were kept private. Now, it is more accepted for men at Chevron to take on and publicly share caregiver roles.

Another sign was when a male executive who had recently gone through a divorce spoke at an event. He shared that he had never before realized how much mental labor, planning, and logistics were involved in day-to-day parenting. To me, the big deal here wasn't the realization this man had. Plenty of other divorced dads have come to the same conclusion. The big deal was that this executive shared his realization *at work in front of an audience.* The fact that he felt comfortable enough to do so was evidence of broad cultural change at Chevron.

Finally, I'll never forget what happened at an external event when a woman approached me and said, "My company is a contractor with Chevron. At a meeting where I could have been overlooked, a male Chevron employee kept bringing the conversation back to me. Afterward, I thanked him, and he told me that speaking up when he saw exclusionary behavior was a skill he learned in the MARC program."

For me, hearing about the program's success from someone *outside* the company showed that our work really had legs—and that Chevron's reputation for gender equity was growing.

As a side note, we believe that developing a reputation for equity is important to Chevron's ongoing growth. In the talent wars, organizations with a strong cultural reputation will have an advantage, because employees of the future will vote with their feet and gravitate toward employers who share their values.

Reward and recognize those who are doing well. We look for employees who demonstrate allyship and who are living out the gender equity principles they've learned through participating in MARC. When possible, we publicly recognize those employees. People often need "permission" to change their behavior. They need clear examples to show them what right looks like.

Gather employee feedback and act on it. In addition to surveying employees about aspects of Chevron's culture, we survey MARC participants on the program itself. *How are we doing? What are we learning? What needs to change?*

For example, during the pilot we surveyed groups each month on what they thought needed to change in Chevron's culture. One of the most common pieces of feedback we received from men was that there was no paternity leave, which was a barrier to gender equity in the workplace. As a direct result, Mike Wirth and other senior leaders took action by instituting eight weeks of bonding time for all new parents, regardless of gender.

If you gather employee feedback, it's crucial to act on it (or, in some cases, explain why their request isn't possible). If you don't, employees will quickly cease to engage in your change initiative.

Look for new opportunities when you encounter challenges. When the pandemic began, MARC's small group meetings had to go digital. Rather than using this as an excuse to back away or shut down the program, we used the new digital infrastructure as an opportunity to include additional employees—particularly those in smaller or more remote locations. Post-pandemic, we continue to focus on recruiting MARC participants from field settings like operations and maintenance, which typically have more male employees than female employees.

Final Thoughts

While our MARC program is focused on gender equity, the best practices and skills we've shared are highly transferable and adaptable. They can be used to facilitate all types of culture change within organizations. In fact, within Chevron, this blueprint is seen as the way to make change of any kind happen.

The Win, Build, Send model works so well because it fosters authentic relationships, which are the key to managing change in an uncertain business world. They lead to workplace satisfaction, collaboration, innovation, adaptability, and performance.

9

Bring Humanity to Work

5 B's of Gender Partnership

- ⊘ Begin with You
- ⊘ Break Down What's Not Working
- ⊘ Build Up What's in It for Men
- ⊘ Bridge the Gender Gaps
- ⊘ **Bring Humanity to Work**

Our colleagues come from different backgrounds and may have vastly different experiences and viewpoints from our own. But we are all connected by our humanity. Gender partners bring empathy and build empowering environments in which people can be their authentic selves and lead in ways that serve the organizations best, regardless of gender.

The final B is Bring Humanity to Work; if we don't interact with respect and dignity, we create a climate of silence or a combative culture driven by fear.[1] To generate a culture of inclusion—which ultimately results in a strong, thriving organization—we must aspire to lead with our humanity.

CEO = Chief Empathy Officer

As work has become predominantly digital, especially with the ascension of artificial general intelligence, there has been increasing focus on the uniquely human aspect of empathy as a critical leadership skill. At Catalyst, we talk about empathy as a superpower in the future of work[2] and why it's especially important during times of crisis.[3] Here's what empathy looks like in a real-world work scenario.

Jonathan, a senior executive in Europe, told me, "I would describe my leadership style as having a lot of female characteristics." While he was a little hesitant to use this language (he acknowledged that "it's stereotypical as well"), he went on to name these "feminine" qualities as "good listening skills and seeking to understand other people's perspectives."

Since traditional ideas of femininity and leadership have been—wrongly—regarded as incompatible in the past,[4] this was a remarkable statement. It became clear to me that Jonathan considers his leadership style an asset, not a liability. In other words, he proudly embraces his empathy.

But he has also discovered that being an empathetic leader has "caused some problems" because "my empathy and ability to feel and embrace situations can be interpreted as a lack of tough decision-making. Yet, in fact, I actually make tougher decisions than many of my colleagues do! This is overlooked because I'm not a person who pounds his chest."

Despite misconceptions like those Jonathan has experienced, embracing empathy is one of the traits that makes him an effective leader. In fact, empathy is a core leadership characteristic and a crucial workplace skill for all employees.

"Empathy" is a word we hear a lot, and it's one people tend to use in a general way to mean seeking to understand other people's feelings and motivations. At Catalyst, we drill down and talk about three ways to be empathetic: through thinking, feeling, and doing.[5]

- Thinking, or cognitive empathy, is imagining how a colleague is feeling from their unique perspective. Example: If a member of your team fulfilled an assignment differently from the way you expected, and you believe the result is inadequate, thinking about it from their perspective could mean that instead of assuming they didn't understand the instructions, or didn't care, you would consider the reasons they made the decisions they did and try to understand if their approach made sense to *them*.

- Feeling, or affective empathy, involves experiencing concern for a colleague. If a colleague tells you that they will have to miss an important meeting because, for instance, they need to have surgery that day, your first instinct would be to worry about their health, not express annoyance that now you have to take their place.

- Doing, or behavioral empathy, means demonstrating active listening and a desire to understand more about a colleague's feelings, experiences, or reactions. For example, if a colleague confides in you that they lack confidence in public speaking and they are dreading an upcoming presentation, you might practice active listening, paraphrasing their concerns so that you can check for understanding and make sure they feel heard, and use nonverbal cues like head nodding to communicate empathy with their circumstances.

All three of these elements of empathy are important, and practicing them can help bond colleagues together. Although it is often underestimated as a business skill, mastering empathy skills is, as Catalyst findings suggest, a business imperative and essential to success.[6]

The converse is true as well: Avoiding empathy in the name of being "tough" is an ineffective form of leadership.[7] Jonathan explains this brilliantly: "If you report to someone who elevates being tough and competitive and brutish, do you really speak up if you have a different point of view, a different perspective? No, you won't." And companies do not succeed unless leadership hears multiple points of view.

Catalyst surveyed nearly 900 US employees working across industries to understand the effects of empathetic leadership on their experiences at work, and we found that empathy is an important driver of employee outcomes such as innovation, engagement, and inclusion—especially in times of crisis or rapid change.[8] For example, the percentage of employees with high levels of innovation more than quadruples when senior leaders demonstrate empathy; and the percentage of those with a high level of engagement more than doubles. We also found that women from marginalized racial and ethnic groups experience less burnout when they have more empathetic senior leaders.

Additionally, senior leader empathy is linked to employee retention. Women with empathetic leaders who respect their life circumstances and seek to understand and value them as people are less likely to consider leaving the company. Empathetic leadership is a key driver of inclusive workplaces that support employees' work and life needs, two important factors of employee retention. Being intentional and taking the time to connect with team members to understand their experiences and show care and concern is critical to inclusion, retention, and other positive employee experiences, especially for women of color.

A few years ago, to raise awareness of the importance of empathy in the workplace, Catalyst launched an impactful campaign for International Women's Day in which we encouraged leaders to embrace the role of CEO—Chief Empathy Officer. Partnering with *The CEO Magazine*, we created personalized CEO (Chief Empathy Officer) magazine covers, which members of the Catalyst community shared on their social media platforms.[9] One of the fulfilling outcomes of this campaign was that men as well as women participated. Seeing men pasting their headshots into the *CEO Magazine* cover template we created demonstrated not only that empathy is a necessary workplace skill but also that everyone, regardless of gender, needs it to succeed. Empathy, in short, is not inherently feminine. Rather, it is human, and it delivers results. Jonathan has risen to a top executive role in multiple global organizations, despite struggles along the way with other leaders who did not respect Jonathan for his "feminine" leadership style. Wisely, by breaking out of the man box and embracing empathy, Jonathan has created an inclusive culture where everyone—men and women—feels seen and heard, and where women advance to the highest levels of leadership because they, like Jonathan, are valued for who they are, not for conforming to outdated gender stereotypes.

Men in leadership roles: I encourage you to emulate Jonathan. Embrace empathy. To be an effective gender partner, demonstrate to your team the full range of human expression. Challenge the rigid rules of masculinity that form the walls of the man box.

Reimagining Masculinity

Listening to Jonathan, I was struck by his ability to reject traditional masculinity and the man box. (Ironically, going against expectations of how men are "supposed" to behave at work is a very tough and brave thing to do—just as traditional masculinity itself is about being tough and brave!) Instead of thinking about "masculinity" as if it were one thing everyone agrees on, we should instead emphasize the multiplicity of ways that men can behave and exist in their daily lives and in connection with others.

At Catalyst, we use the term *flexible masculinities* to describe moving away from a fixed concept of masculinity and instead embracing a *full range* of human characteristics, emotions, and behaviors. There is no single "right" way to be a man, any more than there is a single "right" way to be a woman, and social environments that encourage flexibility—rather than rigidity—allow everyone to thrive. We should all feel supported in embodying a full spectrum of human characteristics and behaviors, whether they are stereotypically masculine, feminine, or somewhere else on the continuum. When we do this, employees, leaders, and organizations can flourish.[10]

Our recent research, with over 5,000 men from 9 countries and more than 12 industries, shows that the overwhelming majority of men very much want a more flexible vision of masculinity:

- 75% of men don't feel like their authentic selves when they're expected to be aggressive, independent, and competitive at work.
- 87% of men want it to be more acceptable to express traits like empathy and kindness in their workplaces.

These data points are a sign that many men want a workplace centered on *humanity*, not gendered stereotypes. However, messages about how men should behave in the workplace discourage them from taking action. Catalyst data on men from Australia, Canada, Europe, and the United States demonstrates that pressure to conform to harmful stereotypes about masculinity is linked to men's decreased engagement in initiatives to create fair outcomes for employees regardless of gender.[11] More key findings include:

- 82% of men experience pressure to conform to stereotypes about masculinity at work, and nearly one in three (29%) report high levels of pressure to conform.
- Addressing stereotypes about masculinity and the ways they box men into a narrow range of "acceptable" behaviors at work is essential for boosting men's participation in organizational efforts to drive fair outcomes for everyone.

No matter how robust your organization's initiatives are to create fairness and equality for men and women, they are doomed to be ineffective if men don't feel they can participate without losing status. These men must be given the opportunity to express the parts of themselves that don't align with traditional masculine stereotypes at work—when they are expected to be aggressive, independent, and competitive to be considered successful.[12]

Meet Everyone's Human Needs (Regardless of Gender)

Gavin, a senior leader who participated in one of our MARC programs, opened up to us about wanting the ability to leave the office at the end of the official workday.[13] Rather than being expected to stay late as a matter of course, he wanted to care for his young children during that time. Gavin recalled getting dirty looks and passive-aggressive questions and comments about his desire to leave at the end of the standard workday, and he felt that people completely delegitimized his needs for flexibility because he was a man.

The default assumption was that men can work long hours day after day because they aren't responsible for childcare, even if they have young children. What he experienced was gender bias—the assumption that men are providers, women are caretakers, and each gender should be treated differently based on these presuppositions.[14]

Gavin went on to tell us that once when he was conducting an online job interview, the candidate asked Gavin and his colleague about work-life balance at the organization. Immediately after the question was asked, they lost their internet connection, and Gavin recalled his colleague joking, "Glad I didn't have to answer that question!" Gavin felt like he was expected to laugh along and agree, but instead, this incident made him feel even more on guard and unsafe about openly discussing his own need to be available to his family during non-working hours. Eventually, Gavin left the organization, making sure to specifically ask about balance and flexibility during interviews with his next company. In that new role, he now regularly checks in on both men and women and ensures they are able to manage a schedule that works with their life circumstances instead of assuming that the issue is relevant only to women with children.

Leaders of successful companies treat employees as human beings with human needs. Genpact president and CEO Balkrishan "BK" Kalra told me that at Genpact they "believe the behaviors that truly drive success are curiosity, courage, and inclusiveness, on a bedrock of integrity. These aren't tied to any gender or group—they're tied to how people think, collaborate, and solve problems." Masculine stereotypes are not part of the equation. Instead, create a work culture that values human traits that everyone can tap into within a culture of inclusion.

Similarly, Chobani founder and CEO Hamdi Ulukaya also prioritizes treating employees as whole humans—a value that is of particular importance considering the makeup of the company's workforce: hundreds of Chobani employees are refugees and immigrants. Hamdi told us,[15]

When I started Chobani, we hired everyone we could in the local community in upstate New York. But we were growing so quickly, I needed more help. Local refugee centers knew people who needed work. Being an immigrant myself, I knew firsthand how much people who come to this country take pride in their work. When you come to America, you're so grateful to be here and to have this opportunity, you just want to contribute. So we hired them.

Now our plants are like the United Nations. Chobani employees come from every conceivable background—our differences make the team stronger and faster. They bring new ideas and perspectives and drive innovation. And you see this everywhere at Chobani. I'm so proud of this.

I don't think of our approach as supporting diversity or equity. It's giving opportunity for people who will do something wonderful with it. That's putting humanity first. And that's in Chobani's DNA.

Investing in your most valuable asset—people—is the most important thing you can do. Your business succeeds even more when employees know their company is invested in their success and well-being.

Business leaders need to build and foster a culture that welcomes everyone. At Chobani, that means everyone can be themselves and not pretend to be someone else. But even with that culture in place, I feel an obligation to do better. Fundamentally, we are all human beings who should draw strength from our differences, not [create] division.

Gavin and Hamdi are both gender partners with different life experiences.[16] For Gavin, seeking a job that allowed him to go home at the end of the day to care for his children after previously being denied this flexibility opened his eyes to the necessity of empathy as a leader. For Hamdi, being an immigrant informs his commitment to giving everyone a chance and seeing employees as people first.

Men, no matter what draws you to gender partnership, I hope you know how liberating it is to escape the walls of the man box—to know you can safely admit to your manager when you've made a mistake and you're sorry; to know that if you want or need to, you can rearrange your schedule to take your mom to the clinic or to spend time with your kids before bed; to welcome team members with diverse backgrounds and experiences; or to shed a tear of sadness or happiness, even in front of colleagues.

Now go create this inclusive culture for everyone, for the benefit of all.

Recognize That We Are All Multifaceted

Remember Gerald Lema, from chapter 8, who made a special effort to recruit women in Japan who were on parental leave? Gerald didn't only see the absence of women; he saw the absence of a particular demographic of women—those with young children. This was an intersectional view of the problem his company faced. *Intersectionality* is a framework for understanding how social identities (such as gender, race, ethnicity, sexual orientation, age, social class, religion, caregiver status, etc.) overlap with one another and with systems of power that oppress and advantage people in the workplace and broader community. Coined by legal scholar Kimberlé Crenshaw in 1989, intersectionality enables us to understand different people's varying experiences in the world.[17]

Intersectionality is not a code word for diversity. And it is not about *adding* one aspect of identity to another. Rather, it is about how people with overlapping identities experience systems of power. The Tokyo mothers did not face challenges with reentering the workforce simply as women; they faced challenges as women who were also mothers.

Understanding intersectionality is business-critical for high-performing teams.[18] Leaders need to understand how overlapping identities impact workplace communication, inclusivity, and belonging—all

the things that make employees feel engaged, encourage them to innovate, and inspire them to stay at the company.[19] Here's another example
of intersectionality in action (and also proof that women, too, can see
the world through a biased lens!). Angela, a white senior executive,
attended a MARC workshop and was dismissive when the facilitators
introduced the concept of men having certain advantages over women
simply because they are men.[20] She insisted that she had never experienced being unfairly treated or put at a disadvantage because she was
a woman.

Angela's declaration opened a valve, and multiple responses sprang
out. One woman in the group asked Angela to consider the experiences of women at her company who are more junior or who are women
of color. Others shared examples of how they had either witnessed or
experienced inappropriate or unfair behavior at work. The conference
room where the workshop was taking place became filled with raucous
conversations among women of different backgrounds and organizational levels.

Angela realized that her personal experience was not necessarily shared by other women, and she shouldn't have assumed that all
women are the same. She later said, "We learn to adapt, to be resilient,
and to work around [bias against women] so at some point we no longer
see it. And we don't want our gender to be what we are about. But I
now see that I need to be a better partner for women who are different
from me."

As Angela learned, there is no one single way of experiencing
being a woman. The differences can be especially stark when we look at
race and ethnicity. Gender wage gap data from the United States, for
instance, reveals not just lower pay for women compared to men but
also higher lifetime earning losses for Black women, Latinas, Indigenous women, and many groups of Asian American, Native Hawaiian,
and Pacific Islander (AANHPI) women when compared with white

women.[21] The disparities showcase how racism and sexism interact to create unique inequities.

My own eyes were opened to the multiple ways our identities intersect when I attended the MARC immersive workshop for leaders. One of the activities is called Walk the Line. On the first morning of the two-day program, the two facilitators instructed the three dozen of us in the group to line up on one side of the conference room where the workshop was held. They took turns reading a series of statements. If a statement was true for us (and if we wanted to share that information with the others), we were to move to the other side of the room. It was up to us to choose what to share or not, and it didn't matter how "obvious" we thought the information was to anyone else.

The statements included (among many others):

You've listened to and laughed at demeaning jokes told by men.

You've been told, "I don't think of you as a member of your racial or ethnic group."

At work, someone has implied that you might be getting too old to be up-to-date.

You or your parents were raised in poverty.

You have been a member of a religious community that is not Christian.

You or your parents immigrated to the country you now reside in.

You have hidden a part of your identity in order to fit in, protect yourself, or "pass" at work.

You, or a member of your family, or a close friend, are gay, lesbian, bisexual, or asexual.

You or someone in your family has a physical disability or impairment.

You or a family member has struggled with addiction.

When I chose to walk across the room, it was a powerful experience to see who joined me, and who did not. And it was also powerful to be someone *not* walking across the room and seeing who did, and who did not. We conducted this activity in silence, and the silence, too, was powerful. I was very aware of the multiple life experiences and identities people carry with them—many of them invisible, all of them nuanced. And every single one of us has a unique intersection of experiences of identities that makes us unique.

Social psychologist Corin Ramos, who led Catalyst research on gender, race, and culture, has eloquently explained the reasons that we can't make change in our workplaces until we fully understand intersectionality. I'm including excerpts from her interview because it's the best explanation of intersectionality for a general audience that I've ever read.[22]

Why should leaders care about intersectionality? Since everyone faces challenges in their life based on their identity, doesn't that mean we're all intersectional in our own ways?

Corin Ramos: Focusing on identity is a simplified way of looking at it. You can have multiple identities, but the difference is how those identities are affected by deep-rooted bias. A lot of times, people think of intersectionality as only gender and race intersecting. They forget about things like sexuality, ability, age, immigration status—all these different identities that can interplay.

What is the emotional tax that people of color experience when companies fail to address intersectional identities in the workplace?

Ramos: Catalyst has done a lot of research on *emotional tax at work*.[23] It's about feeling different from the rest of the group and being on guard against potential bias, plus the risks to your well-being that come along with that state. People across intersections of race, ethnicity, gender, and other aspects of identity are vulnerable to these risks. And when their identities and unique challenges or differences are not addressed, they may feel unsafe in the workplace and experience intent to quit their job. High turnover can be a problem for companies with employees who experience emotional tax.

How can leaders create safe and supportive environments for all staff?

Ramos: Culture change comes from the top. Leaders must foster a sense of psychological safety so that their employees feel supported and okay to take risks without penalty or fear of repercussions.[24] Employees should have that open space to suggest new ideas or even discuss difficult topics. Leaders should also strive to create safe environments by facing their own shortcomings head-on. When having difficult conversations, leaders will naturally feel uncomfortable. They shouldn't let this affect their willingness to create safe spaces or have candid conversations about important topics. It is a difficult task, but one with high stakes, especially for people of color.

Nearly all of us know what it's like to feel "othered" due to the facets of ourselves that are different from those around us. We need to draw on that feeling and let it inspire us to reach out to those who might need some support. David Simmonds of Canada Life & Great-West Lifeco told me about the impact of three people—all from underrepresented groups—who mentored him in the early stages of his career. They "would often talk to me about what they saw in me that I couldn't see myself; they gave me permission to be more than I thought I could. And that was powerful; I owe them a debt of gratitude for unlocking the talent in me." As a Black gay man, David benefited from guidance early in his career from people who brought different facets of their own intersectional selves to their mentorship. When your team includes people from underrepresented groups, everyone benefits. Members of those groups bring diverse experiences and opinions and demonstrate to others that they don't have to be a member of the dominant group to succeed. However, it can be lonely when you're a member of one or more underrepresented groups. Having mentors who understand the emotional toll of this can make a huge difference in how you see yourself and where you can grow within your career. Members of dominant groups can, and must, also play a role. David went on to work for three CEOs—all white, straight men. These leaders, who eventually became his sponsors, recognized that David had the potential to be high-performing, and they gave him stretch opportunities. "They put me in roles I was not quite ready for," David recalled, "and they taught me how to succeed, while giving me the freedom to redefine professionalism in a way that makes sense for me. And in so doing, they allowed me to play a role in advancing a culture that felt more open to people from diverse backgrounds."

Both David's mentors and sponsors taught him a crucial lesson: "To advance as diverse leaders we need to be brought into the system so that we can be prepared for leadership. I'm grateful that I was given the tools and the mentors I needed to help me to succeed."

Respect Others' Personal Life Needs

I've mentioned this before, but it's so consequential for gender partnership that it bears repeating: **Men and women alike thrive at work when leaders model work-life integration.**[25] If you are a man, one of the best ways to hold yourself accountable to gender partnership is to show employees that you have a personal life, that you tend to it, that doing so makes you a better person and better leader, and that having employees who respect personal life needs leads to a stronger organization.

Amy Wilson of Dow told me that she will never forget what a male leader said at a meeting shortly after she joined Dow, over 25 years ago. He told the group, "We're going to start and end on time because my son has a basketball game at five o'clock, and I'm not going to miss it." And everyone accepted this as normal.

"I was coming from private law practice," Amy continued. "That wasn't the norm there, to even talk about family, set boundaries, and acknowledge it as important and a priority. So it had an impact on me really early in my career, and it was coming from a male leader, which made it even more powerful, because it meant a lot to hear a male leader make that announcement, set those boundaries. And everybody in the room went, 'Yep, understood.' And, you know, it was not only okay, it was respected, and we finished the meeting on time because of that."

When a leader establishes boundaries and talks about their family or other personal obligations as sacrosanct, it makes a difference. But it's even more impactful when it comes from a male leader, someone who, traditionally, might be the one most likely to enforce traditional gender stereotypes and roles. As a result of that meeting, Amy decided that she was going to do the same thing herself. She, too, would tell her team when she had family or personal commitments. She, too, is a gender partner.

On the flip side, if employees feel they need to hide their personal challenges, this could be a red flag that the workplace culture is not as healthy as it should be. To achieve equality for everyone, people need to trust that they can share their life challenges without experiencing negative repercussions.[26] Amy explains, "Whenever you see that people care a lot about how well your personal life is going, you're so much more inclined to share because they don't use that against you. Obviously, you can't hide a pregnancy, but you might have aging parents, or you might hide other things like a health challenge because you're unsure how they will react."

Emma, an executive at a Canadian financial services company, told me that during the COVID stay-at-home orders, she had two young children and, like nearly all office-based employees, was working from home. Remember how challenging that time was? Even if you personally don't have children, or yours are older, surely you knew parents scrambling as schools and day care centers closed, along with playdates and all the other crucial institutions and relationships that make being a working parent feasible. For moms in particular—even if they had a male partner—this was an incredibly stressful period as people acclimated to video calls with messy, chaotic backgrounds and young ones in another room, or the same room, crying or singing or just making the myriad sounds that kids make.

Emma had two different managers. Both told her to take the time and space she needed with her children, but they had vastly different expectations. Here is how she tells her story:

> It was a really, really challenging two years. My husband and I were both working full-time and we were really on our own for those two years. To make matters worse, I was consumed with a massive strategic project.
>
> I had two leaders who were guiding strategy, and they could hear my kids in the background. I'd be in the middle of a call with all the C-suite execs giving me updates, and I'd have a two-year-old in the background asking to go to the bathroom. Both my leaders said, "Do what you need to do. Take the time you need to take. This is a really difficult time; I can only imagine." But only one demonstrated it with action and gave me the space to work flexibly, even if it meant that I needed to take a

break in the middle of the day, because, you know, my kids can only entertain themselves for so long. [He made it okay to] log off, then log back on at night. That was perfectly fine.

Conversely, the other would say things like, "Yeah, no problem. And also, can you just make sure you have that to me by 5:00 PM?"

It was such a difference. I hold in the highest regard the individual who gave me space and flexibility. And I think it also speaks to what people are willing to do when they have a great leader. I still have an incredible relationship with that particular leader and would gladly go work for them and support them and be a part of their team.

The lesson here is that being a good gender partner is good for business: If you want to build and sustain a high-performance team in which members are committed to getting the job done at the highest levels, you need to care about them as whole people with lives that sometimes can be messy.

Help Employees Feel They Matter and Belong

Several years after she joined Dow, Amy became pregnant. She worried about telling her male manager, and she worried about how her pregnancy would affect the team, which was male-dominated. She strategized that the best way to announce the news was along with a detailed memo about how her work could be handled during her parental leave. When she shared the memo and made the announcement, she was surprised and pleased by her boss's unabashedly positive reaction. Immediately, he congratulated her and gave her a hug. He also told her that it wasn't her job to worry about what would happen during her leave—that it was *his* job.

"I still remember the conference room I was sitting in, how he pushed my memo away and said, 'If anyone makes you feel like this is anything but a good thing, you tell them to come talk to me,'" she remembers. "It was such a powerful moment, in part because it was unexpected, but primarily because of how genuine he was, and the tone that he set for the whole team. It was a big leadership lesson for me."

Amy's boss was a gender partner because he not only set up Amy for success during her pregnancy and parental leave but also because he set up everyone on the team for success by showing that being inclusive means not only ensuring that everyone is treated fairly and respectfully but also recognizing that significant life events impact both men and women.

Whenever you're in a situation like Amy's boss and you want to be inclusive but you're not sure how, think of these words, which cofounder and managing partner at Navalent Ron Carucci told me. He said every single person in the workplace shows up every single day with these questions on their mind:

> *Do I matter; is my contribution valued?*
> *Do I belong; am I welcome here?*
> *Is the work I do connected to some larger outcome?*
> *Do I have as much of a chance of being successful as anybody else here, no matter how I show up?*

"If people know the answer to these questions is yes, all of their capacity goes into their job and performance," Ron said. "The minute an employee starts to doubt whether the answers are yes, they stop performing and begin *pretending* to care. So, as a leader, you get to decide if you will create an environment where no one doubts they matter. But if people come to work every day investing all their energy into *proving* that they belong, then they're not solving your problems, driving revenue, or growing your company. Instead, they are focusing on making sure their needs to appear like they matter and belong are met."

Leaders have an enormous opportunity and obligation: to be a voice of inclusion; to create an environment in which everyone thrives; and to ensure that employees feel they are valued. In other words, to act as a true gender partner.

CONCLUSION
The Transition from Allyship to Gender Partnership

The workplace of the future is here, and it demands action. The concepts, tactics, and skills described in this book are aimed at creating a fair and inclusive culture marked by the transition from allyship to gender partnership. The combination of external macro forces and internal workforce shifts is making this transition mandatory, and the recommendations need to be infused into strategic initiatives, implemented at every level, and emphasized in leader training.

In fact, our newest Catalyst data, compiled in collaboration with the Meltzer Center on Diversity, Inclusion, and Belonging in 2025, demonstrates that companies that retreat from diversity and inclusion efforts, including those focused on women, do so at their own risk. Executives, leaders, and employees all support the values and benefits of continued commitment and progress. This data shows that a clear majority of C-suite and legal leaders say that, in the past, their organization has seen a positive correlation between its diversity and inclusion programs and employee attraction and retention, and that this will continue over the next few years. Meanwhile, 76% of employees say they are more likely to stay with their employer in the long term if they continue to support these initiatives. Conversely, more than two out of every five employees (43%) say if their employer doesn't continue to support these programs, they'll quit—and this is felt even more strongly by women and the youngest generations in the workplace.[1]

Organizations that retreat risk paying the price with reduced talent retention, adverse financial impact, and negative legal consequences. This is a business imperative: Practices of inclusion create and nourish a culture that will become your competitive advantage.

External Macro Forces Demand Change

Let's look at the big picture. Today's global landscape is changing fast. The population is aging rapidly. In many parts of the world, including the United States, older employees are delaying retirement, and age-diverse workplaces are becoming the norm. But given global demographic realities, there are simply fewer people entering the workforce. At the same time, companies across sectors are growing and changing—and they need talent.[2]

Meanwhile, women are rising. The share of women participating in the labor force is increasing,[3] and they're entering it more educated and career-focused than ever before. Young women in the US are now more educated than men, outpacing the share of men with college degrees (47% versus 37%, respectively).[4] Also, women are poised to control up to 75% of discretionary consumer spending by 2028.[5] In short, women have increased their economic influence and spending power.

The implication is obvious: If a leader wants to attract and retain talent in this climate, it's vital to create a workplace that's attractive to today's generation of talent—both women and men.

As Jim Fitterling, Chair and CEO of Dow, put it:

Look at how many countries are in this world. Very few have birth rates that are currently going to support population growth. And there are low unemployment rates in many parts of the world. You need to attract people in.

You have to create a workplace that's inviting and inclusive for people, and you have to realize, "Whatever I think about what that looks like, there's a whole generation coming up that will sit in this chair someday that thinks it looks a little bit differently." And they're going to vote with their feet. And if it doesn't feel inviting or inclusive to them, they'll go work somewhere else.

The US is just a few years away from becoming a country where racial and ethnic groups that have historically been in the minority will represent the majority of the population.[6] We work in an increasingly geographically dispersed yet globally integrated world. If your people aren't prepared to work productively and inclusively in diverse environments, your ability to be innovative and competitive in the marketplace will be severely limited.

Cultural Workplace Shifts Bring Gender Partnership to the Forefront

Now let's turn inward—inside our organizations. The scope and pace of business has increased dramatically to keep up with a rapidly changing global marketplace. We have to learn faster, evolve our skill sets, create efficiencies, and leverage collective talent across vast organizational networks. In short, the way we work together—men, women, everyone—really matters.

Gender partnership elevates the level of teamwork required to be competitive in this environment. Companies that invest in it can gain huge advantages. Constructing cultures where people across gender feel included creates better places to work. It engages people, builds job satisfaction and trust, and fosters the feelings of belonging and well-being that today's employees value. All of this sets up companies to attract the best talent—and convince them to stay.[7]

As we discussed in chapter 1, diversity and inclusion supercharge innovation, problem-solving, and team performance. Why? Because diverse, inclusive teams tap into multiple perspectives, think more holistically and creatively, and communicate better. This leads to better ideas and faster execution.

And, importantly, it leads to stronger relationships. Strong relationships lead to robust teams and successful companies.[8]

Breaking Out of the Man Box

Along with this emphasis on relationships, we're seeing changing expectations around gender. With younger generations in particular, gender roles and the expectations that go along with them are becoming less traditional.[9] They recognize that rigid, stereotypical ideas around masculinity and femininity don't serve anyone well and should have little (or frankly, nothing) to do with how successful someone can be at work. For decades, women have been struggling to fit into a mold of what successful leadership has looked like historically, and in this book, we show that men have been doing the same. It's important to disrupt expectations for all people.

"Although the pervasiveness of masculinity norms can give men an upper hand in the workplace," notes psychologist Adam Stanaland, "I wonder whether men are contorting themselves to fit into outdated molds of who succeeds at work. Indeed, research shows that successful organizations promote a healthy mix of stereotypically masculine and feminine qualities." Stanaland's research demonstrates that—contrary to gender stereotypes—men develop "fragile masculine identities" when they feel pressured to live confined within the man box. He concludes that "it's best when people of *all* genders feel comfortable showcasing traits such as cooperation and agency."[10]

Likewise, the research Catalyst has been doing for over 15 years shows again and again that gender partnership is possible when the workplace culture is inclusive to all. On the other hand, when the workplace culture promotes inflexible ideas about what it means to "be a man" and equates "being a man" with success, it becomes harder to create gender partnerships.[11]

The Roadmap to Gender Partnership

Creating the conditions that help employees, teams, and companies thrive calls for a different kind of leader. This is truer than ever in the age of AI (artificial intelligence). As Paul Hudson, CEO of health care company Sanofi, shared with a room full of C-suite executives at a 2025 Catalyst conference: "We actually don't have a choice in our collective evolution as leaders. As AI becomes widely used, creating less dependence on human IQ, it leaves EQ [emotional quotient, or emotional intelligence] as the required competitive advantage in our workplaces."

The expectations of leadership have moved toward a broader, more "human" spectrum and away from the traditional "masculine" versus "feminine" traits that keep us (falsely) separate. At Catalyst, we recognize the need for "durable skills," like empathy, humility, and vulnerability. We encourage evolving the term "soft skills" because that plays into a stereotype about women's leadership, and besides, there's nothing "soft" about essential skills that everyone needs to succeed in senior roles. These skills are embedded in the 5 B's to gender partnership we've laid out in this book: Begin with You; Break Down What's Not Working; Build Up What's in It for Men; Bridge the Gender Gaps;

and Bring Humanity to Work. These are not just "nice ideas"—they are the essential human skills for the future of work. As younger generations rise through the ranks, the outdated and divisive narrative will finally lose its grip.

Ultimately, we are rewriting the rules. We are redefining what leadership looks like—free from the constraints of gender stereotypes—so we can adapt, be resilient, and be competitive in a new world. This more expansive view creates workplaces where inclusion isn't a sideline conversation but a central strategy, where talent and trust are the cornerstones of success, and where leadership is fully human.

Now is the time. Let's join forces to accelerate progress for women, free men from the burden of traditional masculine stereotypes, and create workplaces where everyone can thrive and grow. We will create the roadmap for a better future together.

APPENDIX
GETTING TO KNOW MARC[1]

Catalyst's **MARC™** (Mutual Accountability, Real Change) inspires leaders at all levels to leverage their unique opportunity and responsibility to be advocates for fair and inclusive workplaces. MARC is about effective gender partnership—which can only be achieved by bringing everyone to the table.

The MARC initiative is about equipping people of all genders with the skills to be more effective partners and to lead from a place of personal conviction and understanding. Through creating personal connections and unpacking root causes, MARC participants work hard to understand, identify, and address gender gaps and other critical elements of workplace fairness and inclusion.

So what does a typical MARC journey look like? In short, there is no such thing—each organization has its own point of departure, its own challenges and strengths, and its own unique pathway for implementing different MARC learning programs. However, we have noted some common success factors among organizations that have implemented MARC. Read on to learn about five of these factors, gathered from the lessons learned and best practices of MARC client organizations from multiple industries around the world.

Success Factors:

1. A Strategic Approach: Who, What, and Why

WHO:

While many organizations are committed to fairness and inclusion as a strategic business imperative, they are faced with two challenges. For one, gaps persist, and progress to close them has slowed or even stalled. At the same time, efforts to close gender gaps and drive progress toward more fair and inclusive workplaces for all has resulted in some employees—namely men—feeling left out and left behind.

MARC is committed to addressing both sides of this equation—helping organizations to close critical gaps that hinder progress and empowering all employees, regardless of gender, to feel welcome and act as agents of change.

Organizations that engage in MARC work create spaces for learning that invite everyone into the conversation, equipping them with the knowledge, confidence, and skills to act as partners in jointly shaping a fair, inclusive, and productive path forward. Through MARC's gender partnership approach, everyone has a role to play—for their own benefit, for the benefit of others, and ultimately for the benefit of the business.

At P&G, MARC addresses not just how the company wants to change its culture, but *who* is responsible for driving this change. MARC participants ask themselves, "What conversations are we having? Who is accountable for inclusion, and how do we approach it?" MARC has been a tool for bringing leaders from different business areas together to move forward as a corporate community.

Building on this, many MARC clients have successfully framed their MARC strategy as a business imperative focused on leadership development rather than an effort that is separate from the core business. Likewise, the MARC framework for gender partnership provides both an entry point and an anchor for knowledge, empathy, and the development of new skills that are relevant for all business areas.

MARC presents both an opportunity to learn—for example to uncover knowledge gaps and implicit associations—and a chance to share personal experiences with their colleagues, helping to build empathy and bridge divides.

> I came here today thinking, *What am I doing here? This has nothing to do with me.*
>
> *I was brought up being told I can achieve anything I want and I don't feel like a victim.*
>
> But I heard my colleagues' statements. I talked to other participants.
>
> And it became quite emotional . . . It was a real eye-opener for me.
>
> You taught me differently and I'm grateful for that.
>
> —Woman Leader

WHAT:

Once a company has committed to using MARC as a strategic approach, the next step is deciding which program(s) to leverage. While there are many possibilities, the basic structure depends on whether the company would most benefit from a top-down or a bottom-up approach.

Top-Down

Companies that have taken a leadership-first approach have centered around a commitment to put a critical mass of global leaders through immersive MARC learning.

At one financial company, senior leaders had already made a strong commitment to inclusion. However, the company also chose the top-down approach to provide senior leaders with deeper insight into root causes as well as strategies to cascade actionable learning throughout the organization. Through teach backs and dialogue with their teams, these leaders influence change by increasing the sense of workplace belonging among employees, as well as improving recruiting and employee-development practices.

At a retail banking company, influential managing directors from around the globe participated in the initial MARC work. These leaders had a profound effect on the corporate culture as they added momentum to the growing inclusion conversation across the organization.

Bottom-Up

The bottom-up approach has worked well in particular across male-dominated industries—for example, at Chevron and other global energy and engineering companies. These organizations recognized an opportunity to open the dialogue at all levels, inviting everyone to engage in building a new collective vocabulary and establishing a shared accountability for driving change.

These companies started by engaging a core group of leaders in deeper learning so they could shape the path for the rest of the organization and support a sustainable, grassroots approach. They then leveraged the MARC Dialogue Teams program to infuse MARC learning across the organization. As Mike Wirth, CEO of Chevron, shared at the MARC Summit:

> Every organization is in a different place on their journey. I think it's important to tailor the approach to where a company is, to tailor to their culture. So, my advice would simply be to assess where you are on the journey. There are different ways to do this—decide where you need to focus. The Women's Network is the one that drove MARC in an effort to reach

out to their male colleagues and engage the men as opposed to the men sometimes sitting on the sidelines on this issue. So, MARC has really become a powerful enabler for inclusion in Chevron. An industry like ours has been historically male dominated—it's really important to get the men involved. We've got several thousand people involved in these [MARC dialogues] with active programs on every continent, but it really has been a grassroots-driven and leaders-supported effort to engage our workforce broadly.

Why:

The MARC suite of learning programs offers something for employees at all levels, including short online training that lays a foundation of understanding, immersive learning experiences for leaders, and everything in between. This range of approaches allows for different entry points, so before a company can choose which path to take, it must assess where it stands in its inclusion journey.

For some companies, MARC is the next step for a successful inclusion program—a natural progression to bring everyone into the conversation to accelerate change and broaden impact. At many organizations, the experiential learning approach of the MARC Leaders Immersive is particularly appealing as it allows participants to explore core principles of inclusion, identify barriers and tailwinds, and challenge assumptions. This opportunity to dive deep both intellectually and emotionally is important for leaders as they take ownership of their learning and practice. Participants describe MARC as creating the foundation for a climate of change.

Other companies choose a MARC program in response to the current moment. Leaders are in search of support as they answer the call to champion change within their own organization. To lead credibly and authentically, they must build a personal connection to the issues at hand by engaging in honest self-reflection and creating a safe space to truly hear others and be heard. For these organizations, MARC presents the means to meet these challenges head-on.

On the other end of the spectrum are the companies who choose a MARC program as an opportunity to create demand. These organizations recognize that their progress has stagnated, in part because some leaders don't yet see themselves as both part of the problem and part of the solution. In those cases, the decision to adopt MARC is often thanks to the investment of a few forward-thinking leaders who make the courageous commitment to leap into deep learning and to bring their colleagues along with them in that process.

There is no right reason to start MARC, but knowing your starting point and setting and communicating appropriate expectations is a must.

> What I always like to say when we're talking about these programs . . . is, "I'm sorry, and you're welcome," to people who go through this journey with us. Because as soon as you start to really gain that awareness and you go along that pathway, you can't stop seeing all of the things that perhaps you just didn't notice before. So, I'm sorry, because now you're seeing it everywhere. And then the acknowledgment that there is usually gratitude for that awakening.
> —Inclusion Leader, Global Pharmaceutical Company

2. A Shared Vocabulary and Courageous Conversations

Much of MARC learning is rooted in dialogue: facilitating conversations about topics that people don't usually talk about at work. Participants commit to really diving into these challenging conversations and not shying away from the sticky questions, healthy disagreement, and sometimes uncomfortable dialogue around the deeply rooted issues that contribute to fairness gaps. However, participants must accomplish this in a way that is nonconfrontational, grounded in research, and brought to life through heartfelt personal examples and reflections.

Participants establish a common framework and vocabulary and learn to talk *with* one another—not at or past one another. They are expected to examine their assumptions and knowledge gaps from a place of humility, and they are equipped with the language and skills to engage in impactful dialogue that can lead to meaningful breakthroughs.

It's essential to enter into MARC programs with a learning mindset and an openness to being pushed outside your comfort zone. Many senior participants have commented on this aspect of MARC programming:

> Attending a MARC Leaders Workshop affects leaders in different ways. For me, it was transformational. I always thought I was rather enlightened in my attitudes towards gender equity. Through MARC, I realized [. . . I] *was only scratching the surface.* I wasn't getting it wrong; I just wasn't getting it all. It is not enough just to say "I am for gender equity." To be an effective leader of a diverse workforce, I must make a deliberate, continuous effort to deeply understand the dynamics involved, engage in dialogue, and then act.
>
> —Executive, Global Manufacturing Company

> Men now have some language and insight that they can work with and they now have a stake in the success of diversity and inclusion. They think, *I am a part of this, and I stand to benefit from this.* It was MARC who introduced that to us. And, after having gone through

the program, women have also come back and said that they didn't realize there is so much in MARC for them, specifically, a deeper understanding of diversity and inclusion. Our female leaders are inspired to partner with their male colleagues to lift up the culture of the entire organization. The introduction of critical concepts invites an ongoing conversation. So right away a small stone of new language, new understanding, and new attention is dropped into the company's cultural pool.

—Leader, Global Consumer Goods Company

3. Vulnerability and Safety

MARC is an invitation to learning, self-reflection, and dialogue. This involves establishing an environment of safety that enables participants to share openly and honestly and build emotional connections.

As one leader at a chemicals company reflected, MARC doesn't simply tell its participants that the workshops are safe spaces for emotional vulnerability—the program actually demonstrates how a safe environment feels. And as people realize that vulnerability is not a weakness but a strength, they drop their masks—if not during the workshops, then during the weeks and months that follow. Employees have reported becoming more assertive, confident, and outspoken as advocates since participating in MARC.

MARC meets people where they are and allows them to grow from there. Long after workshops have ended, employees continue to embrace this approach to partnering with their colleagues.

MARC is a safe and helpful way to give everyone the opportunity to discover how their personal experiences, views, and opinions might provide an incomplete picture of the world around them, and how filling out those perspectives is fundamental to change.

A global bank implemented MARC training and practices across their international corporate communities in the UK, Singapore, and India. The bank also used the opportunity to engage its clients, and many participants commented on the importance of having these conversations in the workplace.

One large global manufacturing company reports that MARC has helped develop its culture and make it stronger. As one leader shared, MARC takes a very intimate approach, which creates a great learning dynamic. The individual focus and the emphasis on creating personal connections to the content helped their leadership internalize this practice. One senior executive reported that he was happy that he was asked to focus on emotional tools as well as practical tools because reframing actions isn't procedural—it's relational and emotional.

4. Leadership Commitment

Senior leadership support is one of the most effective factors that enables an organization to move forward in its MARC journey. Companies need leaders who not only talk the talk—verbally expressing their support for engaging in MARC work—but who walk the walk by dedicating their own time to complete workshops as engaged participants, setting aside all other work and committing visibly and vocally to learning alongside their colleagues.

At a large global manufacturing company, senior leaders set the tone for each of their MARC workshops by acting as the "sponsors" for the sessions. They led by example, often sharing personal experiences and generally role modeling the introspection, vulnerability, and courage needed for transformational learning. They also brought local data and local context—clear explanations of how MARC fit into their goals. This enthusiastic endorsement from company leadership was critical in setting up the entire organization for success.

A Canadian utilities company first offered MARC to middle managers but quickly added their leadership circle when they realized that support from senior leadership is the most effective way to spread interest and enthusiasm.

MARC presents an opportunity for reframing good leadership. It's not about getting everything right, or having all the answers, but about demonstrating authenticity and accountability through a process of continued learning. While for some leaders this is liberating, for others it's an uncomfortable step into unfamiliar territory. Either way, leaders who complete the workshop feel better equipped to make an impact, not only because they know more, but because they are more aware of how much they still don't know. This allows them to embrace learning as a part of leadership, which can profoundly change their workplace culture.

5. From Education to Action

The final pillar of successful MARC implementation is about translating learning into commitments and commitments into practice. MARC equips participants with knowledge, skill, empathy, and momentum, but it is up to each individual to bring that to life. MARC client organizations have experienced many different outcomes, from personal transformations to sweeping structural changes. Here are several examples:

One MARC exercise was so impactful for a senior executive in the UK that he made a commitment to ensure, whenever possible, that all meetings include both men and women colleagues so that diverse ideas were always brought to the discussion. He also encouraged his entire staff to create personal accountability for driving an inclusive workplace culture.

The upper management team of a large global manufacturing company found that MARC helped them resolve some of their teams' immediate concerns in real time by offering a safe space where they could effectively resolve these challenges. For example, a team leader had asked an employee to schedule a workshop that ended at 6 PM on a Friday, and while the employee felt that the timing sent the wrong message about work-life balance, she wasn't comfortable saying so. Thanks to the MARC workshop, the team leader realized that he was perpetuating exactly the kind of culture he didn't want—one where people are afraid to speak up. The team collectively committed to ceasing late-Friday meetings, and the leader took the opportunity to examine the group's culture and his own role in building a sense of safety among employees so that they feel they can express their views.

Some companies commit to taking a deeper look at internal policies to assess whether they support or obstruct positive growth and change. For instance, in parallel to MARC, P&G also launched its "Share The Care" initiative, which created a global standard for paid parental leave, establishing a minimum standard of eight weeks fully paid leave for all new parents. Although it originated as an HR policy initiative, many senior business leaders, especially male leaders, many of whom were MARC graduates, supported it. They emphasized P&G's commitment to equal opportunities for all employees and publicly encouraged the adoption of these policies for all employees. This leadership support was crucial for many men, who historically faced expectations to return to work quickly after the birth of a child.

> While participation in MARC Teams is voluntary, its influence at P&G is evident. The business impact of these efforts, both through policy and organizational culture initiatives, has been significant. The MARC program is frequently mentioned in our annual employee survey as a key driver of P&G's inclusive culture. This feedback highlights how MARC initiatives contribute to creating a workplace where respect,

inclusion, and belonging are foundational, enabling all employees to bring their authentic selves to work.

As a global company, these shifts enhance our understanding of our consumers. By considering a broader range of experiences and connecting with deeper insights, we develop new, more relevant solutions that better serve all consumers. This wide range of perspectives is vital for our continued success and business growth.

—Senior Leader, P&G

Thanks to MARC programs, select meetings at a global engineering company now include MARC discussions to inspire compassion, vulnerability, and change. Colleagues who have attended MARC training, including leaders, are using their MARC experiences to help prepare for recruiting, interviewing, and hiring as well as performance reviews.

Many have shared impactful stories on the personal level as well. Partners have reflected that their spouses have gone through transformational changes at home and with their families post-MARC, and colleagues have commented how their bosses are like different people—more open, more aware, more committed, and more inclusive as leaders. Participants themselves share stories of the profound conversations they have engaged in with friends, parents, partners, and children, inspired by MARC to open new dialogues and often surprised and further motivated by what they learn.

The Ongoing Journey

The sometimes elusive but critically important final step in a MARC journey is to sustain momentum. Because any culture-change effort is ongoing and evolving, there is no predetermined end point—instead there must be continued learning and practice. MARC and the broader Catalyst organization can support that through research, resources, further programming, discussion, curated content, and conversations.

For some companies, that means embedding MARC as part of the fabric of the organizational culture, which has been a very successful approach. The challenge and the opportunity is to make gender partnership and shared accountability for advocacy an integral part of workplace culture that infuses the way organizations do business, reward leadership, and approach learning. Consider a three-pronged approach to realizing this goal:

1. Depth: Commit to deep learning. This is not a check-the-box exercise that can be completed in an hour, done just once and never revisited. Embrace and reward learning and dialogue as part of the solution itself—not just a means to an end.

2. Breadth: Reach a critical mass of employees across the company who can cascade learning across the organization. Organizations do not create—or change—culture. People do. The greater the collective engagement in cultural transformation, the greater the impact and potential for sustainable success.

3. Amplification: Talk the talk, walk the walk, and walk the talk. Be visible and vocal about what you are doing both at the organizational and individual level, including the attempts, the learning moments, the successes, and the missteps. Striving for continual improvement and celebrating wins is so important. So, too, is honesty, humility, and vulnerability about the imperfect process that gets you there.

ACKNOWLEDGMENTS

A few years ago, as I was preparing to launch my first book, I remember thinking—and maybe even saying—"If I survive the writing, editing, and promoting of this book, I will never do it again!"

But just like my first childbirth or first marathon, the gift of time creates stronger memories of the positive outcomes, and the pain slowly fades into the background. This book, just like the last one, called me to it, because I knew Catalyst had a unique perspective on a critical workplace topic that hadn't been fully explored and needed to be told. It's a story that shines a light on men, a group too often overlooked in conversations around advancing women, with research-backed insights, practical tools, and powerful stories. And it calls on all of us in leadership to engage as "gender partners" to create change that drives workplace fairness and inclusion for all.

When I embarked on my new job as CEO of Catalyst in the spring of 2024, I was overwhelmed by the treasure trove of thought leadership that Catalyst had on the topic of men dating back to 2009, when, after nearly five decades of focusing on women in the workplace, Catalyst committed to understanding the role that men play as critical agents of change. As our research evolved over more than a dozen years, so did our insight, guidance, and programming. I couldn't imagine a better topic for the first Catalyst book in more than 30 years.

The consistent leader of our expertise in this work has been Alix Pollack, Catalyst's Vice President of Solution Development. She was not only the spark behind the concept of "gender partnership," she has emerged as a leading voice in this space, helping to shape our own understanding and creating tools and training that impact organizations globally. This book simply would not exist without Alix's wisdom, experience, and commitment to this work.

Leora Tanenbaum was the dedicated editor who worked tirelessly with our Catalyst research team and me to ensure that no critical nugget was left unsaid and every detail was factually correct. Over the course of a year, she engaged with an open mind and heart as we wrote and rewrote 60,000+ words, until our deadline forced us to stop. Dottie Dehart was there alongside us, too, our jovial external editor who brought important perspectives and pragmatism required to take 30+ interviews with CEOs and executives and extract the precise stories that would illustrate the key points we hoped would inspire our readers.

Amberlee Wilson kept us organized with meticulous project plans organized in software systems I still can't navigate. She managed our communication, scheduling, legal reviews, endorsements, and the dizzying array of dates to get this book to print and to market on time.

There are hundreds of references in this book, and I love that Catalyst brings credibility with our own data and the external sources we offer. Thank you to Andrew Grissom, Emily Shaffer, and Danielle M. Jackson, who ensured that every citation required was checked, and to Megan Diaz Ellinghaus and James Gaskin, members of our Catalyst legal team, who ensured we had the contracts, legal reviews, and signatures to get this over the finish line.

Matt Holt at BenBella Books took me back as a second-time author, and we gathered the same stellar team around us again. You all make this sound so easy at our kickoff meeting, but you also lean right in and stick with us through every phase of the process, even when it feels overwhelming.

Scott Miller, cofounder of Gray & Miller, is our literary agent and book launch consultant. An author of nine books himself, he knows more than anyone about the industry, but nothing gets him more excited than the marketing and promotion process, and he has offered his wizardry to me once again, often via texts at 5:00 AM local time in Salt Lake City with the message, "Time to talk?"

My family continues to cheer me on as an author and speaker, and I give my father, Roy Scherer, all the credit for encouraging my first book. But it is my devoted husband, Chip McCollum, who jumped right into this one. He eagerly volunteered his own stories to demonstrate his evolution as a gender partner, and the early response was so positive that I knew we were onto something important. Chip, your encouragement warms me and your unconditional love fuels me.

My Catalyst executive team has brought great enthusiasm to this project, brainstorming with me how this book can continue to build our brand and impact with our hundreds of supporters today, and thousands more tomorrow. Thank you to Stacey, Leela, Laura, Sayo, and Trenesa.

And finally, to the rest of the Catalyst staff, your commitment to our mission and our supporters inspires me daily.

NOTES

Introduction

1. Sarah DiMuccio, Negin Sattari, Emily Shaffer, and Jared Cline, *Masculine Anxiety and Interrupting Sexism at Work* (Catalyst, April 28, 2021), https://www.catalyst.org/insights/2021/masculine-anxiety-workplace.

2. Kusum Kali Pal, Kim Piaget, Saadia Zahidi, and Silja Baller, *Global Gender Gap Report 2024* (World Economic Forum, June 11, 2024), https://www.weforum.org/publications/global-gender-gap-report-2024; *Women in Business 2025: Impacting the Missed Generation* (Grant Thornton International, March 4, 2025), https://www.grantthornton.com/insights/articles/insights/2025/women-in-business-2025-impacting-the-missed-generation.

3. Amelia Costigan, *The Double-Bind Dilemma for Women in Leadership*, infographic (Catalyst, 2018), last modified February 29, 2024, https://www.catalyst.org/insights/2024/infographic-the-double-bind-dilemma-for-women-in-leadership.

4. *Flexible Masculinities at Work*, infographic (Catalyst, 2023), https://www.catalyst.org/insights/2023/masculinity-rigid-flexible-infographic.

5. *Executive Talking Points for Inclusive Workplaces* (Catalyst, 2025), https://www.catalyst.org/insights/2025/executive-talking-points-inclusion; Dnika J. Travis, Emily Shaffer, and Jennifer Thorpe-Moscon, *Getting Real About Inclusive Leadership: Why Change Starts with You* (Catalyst, November 21, 2019), https://www.catalyst.org/en-us/insights/2019/inclusive-leadership-report.

6. "Educating the Next Generation of Young Boys," panel discussion delivered at the MARC Summit by Catalyst, online conference, December 3, 2020. See these links: https://www.fairplaytalks.com/2020/11/27/2020s-marc -summit-inspires-men-to-be-advocates-for-equity; https://www.youtube .com/watch?v=oZZzrQd-X7k].

7. *Women in the Workplace 2024: The 10th Anniversary Report* (McKinsey & Company and Leanin.org, 2024), https://www.mckinsey.com/featured -insights/diversity-and-inclusion/women-in-the-workplace; Jenny Donovan, "How Organizations Can Take a Systematic Approach to Pay Equity," Society for Human Resource Management (SHRM), March 11, 2024, https:// www.shrm.org/executive-network/insights/systematic-approach-pay-equity.

8. *Women in the Workplace* (McKinsey & Company and Leanin.org, 2022), https://womenintheworkplace.com/2022; Travis, Shaffer, and Thorpe-Moscon, *Getting Real*; Emily Shaffer and Brittany Torrez, *Promises vs. Progress: 2 Keys to Keeping Employees Feeling Good and Staying Put* (Catalyst, November 21, 2023), https://www.catalyst.org/insights/2023/workplace -DEI-accountability-retention.

9. Alixandra Pollack, David Glasgow, Tara Van Bommel, Christina Joseph, and Kenji Yoshino, *Risks of Retreat: The Enduring Inclusion Imperative* (Catalyst and Meltzer Center for Diversity, Inclusion, and Belonging, June 11, 2025), https://www.catalyst.org/insights/2025/risks-of-retreat-report.

10. *Women in the Workplace 2024* (McKinsey & Company and Leanin.org).

11. Sheila Brassel and Emily Shaffer, *Most Men Support Gender Equity but Face Barriers to Taking Action* (Catalyst, 2025), https://www.catalyst.org/insights /2021/masculine-anxiety-workplace.

12. Daniel A. Cox, "Men's Social Circles Are Shrinking," The Survey Center on American Life, June 29, 2021, https://www.americansurveycenter.org /why-mens-social-circles-are-shrinking.

13. Gary Barker, Caroline Hayes, Brian Heilman, and Michael Reichert, *State of American Men 2023: From Crisis and Confusion to Hope* (Equimundo, 2023), https://www.equimundo.org/resources/state-of-american-men.

14. Dan Witters, "U.S. Depression Rates Reach New Highs," *Good Morning America*, May 17, 2023, via Gallup, https://www.goodmorningamerica .com/wellness/story/depression-rates-us-adults-reach-new-high-gallup -99387994; Mental Health America, "Let's Talk About Men's Mental Health," https://mhanational.org/harrys.

15. "One in 100 Deaths Is by Suicide," World Health Organization press release, June 17, 2021, https://www.who.int/news/item/17-06-2021-one-in -100-deaths-is-by-suicide.

16. "Suicide Data and Statistics," Centers for Disease Control, March 26, 2005, https://www.cdc.gov/suicide/facts/data.html.

17. Matt Krentz, Olivier Wierzba, Katie Abouzahr, Jennifer Garcia-Alonso, and Frances Brooks Taplett, *Five Ways Men Can Improve Gender Diversity at Work* (Boston Consulting Group, October 2017), https://www.bcg.com /publications/2017/people-organization-behavior-culture-five-ways-men -improve-gender-diversity-work.

18. Alixandra Pollack and Geoffrey Kerr, *Engaging Men: Barriers and Gender Norms* (Catalyst, 2022), https://www.catalyst.org/insights/2022/engaging -men-barriers-norms; Emily Shaffer, Negin Sattari, and Alixandra Pollack, *Interrupting Sexism at Work: How Men Respond in a Climate of Silence* (Catalyst, June 9, 2020), https://www.catalyst.org/insights/2020/interrupting -sexism-silence.

19. Pollack and Kerr, *Engaging Men*.

20. Sarah DiMuccio, Negin Sattari, Alixandra Pollack, Sandra Ondraschek-Norris, and Joy Ohm, *Gender Partnership: What, Why, How* (Catalyst, September 8, 2022), https://www.catalyst.org/insights/2022/gender-equity -partnership-tool.

21. Dnika J. Travis, Emily Shaffer, and Jennifer Thorpe-Moscon, *Getting Real About Inclusive Leadership: Why Change Starts with You* (Catalyst, November 21, 2019), https://www.catalyst.org/en-us/insights/2019/inclusive-leadership -report.

22. Bruce Hartford, "Fifty Years On: Looking Back on the Freedom Movement," Civil Rights Movement Archive, adapted from *"Troublemaker": Memories of the Freedom Movement* (Westwind Writers, 2019), https://www .crmvet.org/comm/50years.htm.

23. Martha J. Bailey, Thomas Helgerman, and Bryan A. Stuart, "How the 1963 Equal Pay Act and 1964 Civil Rights Act Shaped the Gender Gap in Pay," *Quarterly Journal of Economics* 139, no. 3 (2024): 1827–1878, https:// www.nber.org/papers/w31332.

24. Sheila Brassel and Corin Ramos, *Intersectionality: When Identities Converge* (Catalyst, 2020), last modified 2025, https://www.catalyst.org/insights /2025/intersectionality-when-identities-converge.

25. Felice N. Schwartz, Margaret H. Schifter, and Susan S. Gillotti, *How to Go to Work When Your Husband Is Against It, Your Children Aren't Old Enough, and There's Nothing You Can Do Anyhow* (Simon & Schuster, 1972).

26. Janet L. Yellen, *The History of Women's Work and Wages and How It Has Created Success for Us All* (Brookings Institution, 2020).

27. Felice N. Schwartz, "Management Women and the New Facts of Life," *Harvard Business Review*, January–February 1989, https://hbr.org/1989/01/management-women-and-the-new-facts-of-life.

28. Jennifer A. Kingston, "Women in the Law Say Path Is Limited by 'Mommy Track,'" *The New York Times*, August 8, 1988, sec. A, p. 15, https://www.nytimes.com/1988/08/08/us/women-in-the-law-say-path-is-limited-by-mommy-track.html.

29. Costigan, *The Double-Bind* (Catalyst).

30. *Women of Color in Corporate Management: Dynamics of Career Advancement* (Catalyst, 1998).

31. *Women of Color in Corporate Management: Opportunities and Barriers* (Catalyst, 1999); *Women of Color in Corporate Management: Three Years Later* (Catalyst, 2002).

Chapter 1

1. Vicki W. Kramer, Alison M. Konrad, and Sumru Erkut, *Critical Mass on Corporate Boards: Why Three or More Women Enhance Governance* (Wellesley Centers for Women's Publications Office, 2006), Report No. WCW 11, https://www.wcwonline.org/vmfiles/WCW11.pdf; *Women Matter: Gender Diversity, a Corporate Performance Driver* (McKinsey & Company, 2007), https://www.mckinsey.com/capabilities/people-and-organizational-performance/our-insights/gender-diversity-a-corporate-performance-driver.

2. Miriam Schwartz-Ziv, "Gender and Board Activeness: The Role of a Critical Mass," *Journal of Financial and Quantitative Analysis* 52, no. 2 (2017): 751–80, DOI:10.1017/S0022109017000059.

3. Young Zik Shin, Jeung-Yoon Chang, Keyeongmin Jeon, and Hyunpyo Kim, "Female Directors on the Board and Investment Efficiency: Evidence from Korea," *Asian Business & Management* 19 (2019): 438–479, https://doi.org/10.1057/s41291-019-00066-2.

4. Aida Sijamic Wahid, "The Effects and the Mechanisms of Board Gender Diversity: Evidence from Financial Manipulation," *Journal of Business Ethics* 159 (2019): 705–725, https://doi.org/10.1007/s10551-018-3785-6; Yaoyao Fan, Yuxiang Jiang, Xuezhi Zhang, and Yue Zhou, "Women on Boards and Bank Earnings Management: From Zero to Hero," *Journal of Banking & Finance* 107 (2019): 105607, https://doi.org/10.1016/j.jbankfin.2019.105607.

5. Susan T. Fiske, Amy J. C. Cuddy, Peter Glick, and Jun Xu, "A Model of (Often Mixed) Stereotype Content: Competence and Warmth Respectively Follow from Perceived Status and Competition," *Journal of Personality and Social Psychology* 82, no. 6 (2002): 878–902, https://doi.org/10.1037/0022-3514.82.6.878; Laurie A. Rudman and Peter Glick, "Prescriptive Gender Stereotypes and Backlash Toward Agentic Women," *Journal of Social Issues* 57, no. 4 (2002): 743–762, https://doi.org/10.1111/0022-4537.00239.

6. *Barbie*, directed by Greta Gerwig (Burbank, CA: Warner Bros. Pictures, 2023), https://www.warnerbros.com/movies/barbie.

7. Costigan, *The Double-Bind* (Catalyst).

8. Carlos Aguilar, "America Ferrera and the 'Barbie' Monologue We All Talked About," *The New York Times*, January 1, 2024, https://www.nytimes.com/2024/01/01/movies/america-ferrera-barbie.html.

9. Sheila Brassel, *Breaking Down Gender Stereotypes That Harm Men at Work* (Catalyst, 2025), https://www.catalyst.org/insights/2025/gender-stereotypes-men-work; Sheila Brassel and Emily Shaffer, *Most Men Support Gender Equity but Face Barriers to Taking Action* (Catalyst, 2025), https://www.catalyst.org/en-gb/insights/2025/men-support-gender-equity-regions.

10. Yellen, *History of Women's Work*.

11. Janet L. Yellen, "So We All Can Succeed: 125 Years of Women's Participation in the Economy" (speech, Providence, Rhode Island, May 5, 2017), Board of Governors of the Federal Reserve System, https://www.federalreserve.gov/newsevents/speech/yellen20170505a.htm.

12. Felice N. Schwartz, *Breaking with Tradition: Women and Work, the New Facts of Life* (Basic Books, 1992).

13. *Flip the Script: Gender Stereotypes in the Workplace—Women*, infographic (Catalyst, 2024), https://www.catalyst.org/en-us/insights/2024/flip-the-script-women-in-the-workplace.

14. Ruchika T. Malhotra, "Women of Color Get Asked to Do More 'Office Housework.' Here's How They Can Say No," *Harvard Business Review*, April 6, 2018, https://hbr.org/2018/04/women-of-color-get-asked-to-do-more-office-housework-heres-how-they-can-say-no.

15. Linda Babcock, Maria P. Recalde, Lise Vesterlund, and Laurie Weingart, "In Mixed-Sex Environments, Women Are More Likely Than Men to Perform Tasks That Do Not Lead to Promotion," *American Economic Review* 107, no. 3 (2017): 714–747, https://www.aeaweb.org/articles?id=10.1257/aer.20141734.

16. Lisa Feldman Barrett and Eliza Bliss-Moreau, "She's Emotional. He's Having a Bad Day: Attributional Explanations for Emotion Stereotypes," *Emotion* 9, no. 5 (2009): 649–658, https://doi.org/10.1037/a0016821; Victoria L. Brescoll and Eric Luis Uhlmann, "Can an Angry Women Get Ahead?: Status Conferral, Gender, and Expression of Emotion in the Workplace," *Psychological Science* 19, no. 3 (2008): 268–275, https://journals.sagepub.com/doi/10.1111/j.1467-9280.2008.02079.x.

17. Teresa J. Frasca, Emily A. Leskinen, and Leah R. Warner, "Words Like Weapons: Labeling Women as Emotional During a Disagreement Negatively Effects the Perceived Legitimacy of Their Arguments," *Psychology of Women Quarterly* 46 (2022): 420–437, https://journals.sagepub.com/doi/10.1177/03616843221123745.

18. Frasca, Leskinen, and Warner, "Words Like Weapons."

19. Feldman Barrett and Bliss-Moreau, "She's Emotional."

20. Hillary Rodham Clinton, interview by Lorraine Hariton, March 12, 2024.

21. *Women in the Workplace 2024* (LeanIn.org and McKinsey & Company).

22. "The Lifetime Wage Gap, State by State," *National Women's Law Center*, February 21, 2025, https://nwlc.org/resource/the-lifetime-wage-gap-state-by-state.

23. "The Lifetime Wage Gap by State for Asian Women," *National Women's Law Center*, February 21, 2025, https://nwlc.org/resource/the-lifetime-wage-gap-by-state-for-asian-women.

24. "The Lifetime Wage Gap by State for White, Non-Hispanic Women," *National Women's Law Center*, February 21, 2025, https://nwlc.org/resource/the-lifetime-wage-gap-by-state-for-white-non-hispanic-women.

25. "The Lifetime Wage Gap by State for Black Women," *National Women's Law Center*, February 21, 2025, https://nwlc.org/resource/the-lifetime-wage-gap-by-state-for-black-women.

26. "The Lifetime Wage Gap by State for Native Hawaiian and Other Pacific Islander Women," *National Women's Law Center*, February 21, 2025, https://nwlc.org/resource/the-lifetime-wage-gap-by-state-for-nhopi-women/.

27. "The Lifetime Wage Gap by State for Latinas," *National Women's Law Center*, February 21, 2025, https://nwlc.org/resource/the-lifetime-wage-gap-by-state-for-latinas.

28. "The Lifetime Wage Gap by State for Indigenous Women," *National Women's Law Center*, February 21, 2025, https://nwlc.org/resource/the-lifetime-wage-gap-by-state-for-indigenous-women.

29. Marianne Cooper and Priya Fielding-Singh, "Younger Women's Experiences Show Gender Equity at Work Isn't Inevitable," *Harvard Business Review*, November 1, 2024, https://hbr.org/2024/11/younger-womens-experiences-show-gender-equity-at-work-isnt-inevitable.

30. Cooper and Fielding-Singh, "Younger Women's Experiences."

31. Emma Hinchliffe and Nina Ajemian, "The Share of Women Running Global 500 Companies Falls to Just 5.6%," *Fortune*, August 5, 2024, https://fortune.com/2024/08/05/the-share-of-women-running-global-500-companies-falls-to-just-5-6.

32. Kiley Hurst, "U.S. Women Are Outpacing Men in College Completion, Including in Every Major Racial and Ethnic Group," Pew Research Center, November 18, 2024, https://www.pewresearch.org/short-reads/2024/11/18/us-women-are-outpacing-men-in-college-completion-including-in-every-major-racial-and-ethnic-group.

33. Emily Field, Alexis Krivkovich, Sandra Kugele, Nicole Robinson, and Lareina Yee, *Women in the Workplace 2023* (McKinsey & Company, 2023), https://www.mckinsey.com/featured-insights/diversity-and-inclusion/women-in-the-workplace.

34. *Driving Better Business Results Through DE&I* (EY, 2023). Available from EY upon request.

35. *Women in the Workplace 2022* (McKinsey & Company and Leanin.org).

36. Shane McFeeley and Ben Wigert, "This Fixable Problem Costs U.S. Businesses $1 Trillion," Gallup Workplace, March 13, 2019, https://www.gallup.com/workplace/247391/fixable-problem-costs-businesses-trillion.aspx.

37. Vincent Berube, Ben Fogarty, Neel Gandhi, Rahul Mathew, Marino Mugayar-Baldocchi, and Charlotte Seiler, "Increasing Your Return on Talent: The Moves and Metrics That Matter," McKinsey & Company, April 15, 2024, https://www.scribd.com/document/750461459/increasing-your-return-on-talent-the-moves-and-metrics-that-matter.

38. Ellie Smith and Tara Van Bommel, *Four Drivers of Frontline Employee Satisfaction and Business Results: United States Spotlight* (Catalyst, 2025), https://www.catalyst.org/insights/2025/four-frontline-drivers.

39. *Women in the Workplace 2024* (LeanIn.org and McKinsey & Company).

40. Nancy M. Carter and Christine Silva, *Pipeline's Broken Promise* (Catalyst, 2010), https://www.techcityuk.com/files/system/files/pipeline-s_broken_promise_final_021710.pdf.

41. Nancy M. Carter and Christine Silva, *Myth of the Ideal Worker: Does Doing All the Right Things Really Get Women Ahead?* (Catalyst, 2011), https://www.theprogresspartnership.com/wp-content/uploads/2017/07/The_Myth_of_the_Ideal_Worker_Does_Doing_All_the_Right_Things_Really_Get_Women_Ahead.pdf.

42. Tara Sophia Mohr, "Why Women Don't Apply for Jobs Unless They're 100% Qualified," *Harvard Business Review*, August 25, 2014, https://hbr.org/2014/08/why-women-dont-apply-for-jobs-unless-theyre-100-qualified.

43. Michelle K. Ryan and S. Alexander Haslam, "The Glass Cliff: Evidence That Women Are Over-Represented in Precarious Leadership Positions," *British Journal of Management*, 16, no. 2 (2005): 81–90, https://doi.org/10.1111/j.1467-8551.2005.00433.x.

44. Michelle Budig and Paula England, "The Wage Penalty for Motherhood," *American Sociological Review* 66, no. 2 (2001): 204–25, https://inequality.stanford.edu/sites/default/files/media/_media/pdf/Reference%20Media/Budig_2001_Lifecourse.pdf.

45. Sarah Jane Glynn, *An Unequal Division of Labor: How Equitable Workplace Policies Would Benefit Working Mothers* (Center for American Progress, May 18, 2018), https://www.americanprogress.org/article/unequal-division-labor.

46. Leila Schochet, *The Child Care Crisis Is Keeping Women Out of the Workforce* (Center for American Progress, March 28, 2019), https://www.americanprogress.org/article/child-care-crisis-keeping-women-workforce.

47. Ryan and Haslam, "The Glass Cliff."

48. Textio, *Language Bias in Performance Feedback* (Textio, July 31, 2024), https://textio.com/feedback-bias-2024.

49. Diana Babineau, "Chatting with . . . Moya Bailey," *Northwestern Magazine* (Fall 2023), https://magazine.northwestern.edu/voices/moya-bailey-misogynoir-racism-misogyny-merriam-webster-digital-apothecary.

50. *#LikeAGirl*, Always, accessed June 4, 2025, https://www.always.com/en-us/about-us/our-epic-battle-like-a-girl; Lauren Greenfield, *Run Like a*

Girl—Commercial, produced by Always, October 25, 2014, video, https://www.youtube.com/watch?v=qtDMyGjYlMg.

51. "Redraw the Balance," *Inspiring the Future*, August 11, 2016, accessed June 4, 2025, https://www.inspiringthefuture.org/redraw-the-balance/.

52. *What Are Implicit Associations?* infographic (Catalyst, 2014, updated 2025), https://www.catalyst.org/en-us/insights/2025/infographic-what-are-implicit-associations.

53. *Do You Know What Gender Inequality at Work Looks Like?* Mayor of London Sadiq Khan, May 14, 2018, video, https://www.youtube.com/watch?v=byq-EH9cR00.

54. *The Business Case for Change*, International Labour Organization, 2019, https://www.ilo.org/sites/default/files/wcmsp5/groups/public/@dgreports/@dcomm/@publ/documents/publication/wcms_700953.pdf.

55. *Gender Partnership Can Change Workplaces, Industries, and the World. Just Ask Mike Wirth of Chevron* (Catalyst, 2024), https://www.catalyst.org/insights/2024/video-gender-partnership-chevron-front-line.

56. Travis, Shaffer, and Thorpe-Moscon, *Getting Real*.

57. Emily Shaffer and Brittany Torrez, *How to Talk About Diversity with Employees to Achieve Your Company's Objectives* (Catalyst, 2024), https://www.catalyst.org/en-us/insights/2024/diversity-messaging.

58. Travis, Shaffer, and Thorpe-Moscon, *Getting Real*.

59. "Quick Take: Why Diversity and Inclusion Matter," Catalyst, June 24, 2020, https://www.catalyst.org/insights/2020/why-diversity-and-inclusion-matter.

60. "Why Diversity and Inclusion Matter," Catalyst.

61. Sundiatu Dixon-Fyle, Celia Huber, María del Mar Martínez Márquez, Sara Prince, Ashley Thomas, and Dame Vivian Hunt, *Diversity Matters Even More: The Case for Holistic Impact* (McKinsey & Company, 2023), https://www.mckinsey.com/featured-insights/diversity-and-inclusion/diversity-matters-even-more-the-case-for-holistic-impact.

62. Shaffer and Torrez, *How to Talk About Diversity*.

63. Sapna Cheryan and Hazel Rose Markus, "Masculine Defaults: Identifying and Mitigating Hidden Cultural Biases," *Psychological Review* 127, no. 6 (2020): 1022–52, https://doi.org/10.1037/rev0000209.

64. Laurie A. Rudman, "Self-Promotion as a Risk Factor for Women: The Costs and Benefits of Counterstereotypical Impression Management," *Journal of Personality and Social Psychology* 74, no. 3 (1998): 629–645, https://doi.org/10.1037/0022-3514.74.3.629.

65. Sheila Brassel, *How to Reduce Gender-Based Hostility in Frontline Workplaces* (Catalyst, 2024), https://www.catalyst.org/insights/2024/reduce-sexist -behavior-frontline-workplace.

66. Brassel and Shaffer, *Most Men Support Gender Equity.*

Chapter 2

1. Jennifer Berdahl, Marianne Cooper, Peter Glick, Robert Livingston, and Joan Williams, "Work as a Masculinity Contest," *Journal of Social Issues* 74, no. 3 (2018): 422–448, https://spssi.onlinelibrary.wiley.com/doi/10.1111 /josi.12289.

2. "The State of Boys," panel discussion delivered at the MARC Summit, hosted by Catalyst, online conference, December 3, 2020.

3. Tony Porter, "A Call to Men," TEDWomen, December 9, 2010 video, https://www.ted.com/talks/tony_porter_a_call_to_men.

4. Andrew Grissom, "When Women Tried to Have It All," *MARC Momentum* newsletter, July 25, 2024.

5. Mark Greene, "The History of 'The Man Box,'" *Medium*, January 15, 2019, https://remakingmanhood.medium.com/the-history-of-the-man-box -e6eed6d895c4.

6. Brian Heilman, Gary Barker, and Alexander Harrison, *The Man Box: A Study on Being a Young Man in the US, UK, and Mexico* (Equimundo and Unilever, 2017), 13, https://www.equimundo.org/resources/man-box-study -young-man-us-uk-mexico.

7. Heilman, Barker, and Harrison, *The Man Box*, 38.

8. Amber L. Hill, Elizabeth Miller, Galen E. Switzer, Lan Yu, Brian Heilman, Ruti G. Levtov, et al., "Harmful Masculinities Among Younger Men in Three Countries: Psychometric Study of the Man Box Scale," *Preventive Medicine* 139 (2020): https://pubmed.ncbi.nlm.nih.gov/32593728/.

9. Heilman, Barker, and Harrison, *The Man Box*.

10. "Study: Men Scoring Higher on 'Man Box' Scale Are Prone to Violence, Mental Illness," *Pittwire*, University of Pittsburgh, August 5, 2020, https:// www.pittwire.pitt.edu/pittwire/features-articles/study-men-scoring-higher -man-box-scale-are-prone-violence-mental-illness.

11. "Study: Men Scoring Higher on 'Man Box' Scale," *Pittwire*.

12. Stephanie Pappas, "APA Issues First-Ever Guidelines for Practice with Men and Boys," *American Psychological Association* 50, no. 1 (2019): https://www.apa.org/monitor/2019/01/ce-corner.

13. Pappas, "APA Guidelines."

14. Boys and Men Guidelines Group, *APA Guidelines for Psychological Practice with Boys and Men* (American Psychological Association, 2018), https://www.dcjs.virginia.gov/sites/dcjs.virginia.gov/files/training-events/8137/copy_of_apa_guidelines_for_serving_boys_and_men.pdf.

15. Gary Barker, Caroline Hayes, Brian Heilman, and Michael Reichert, *State of American Men 2023: From Crisis and Confusion to Hope* (Equimundo, 2023), https://www.equimundo.org/resources/state-of-american-men.

16. Ludo Gabriele, *5 Ways Every Man Can Challenge the Toxic Culture of Masculinity* (Catalyst, February 5, 2020), https://www.catalyst.org/en-us/insights/2020/challenge-toxic-masculinity.

17. Richard Reeves, *Of Boys and Men: Why the Modern Male Is Struggling, Why It Matters, and What to Do About It* (Brookings Institution Press, 2022).

18. "How to Respond to the Man Box," unpublished infographic, Catalyst, 2020.

19. "When Boys Become Boys," video presentation delivered at the MARC Summit by Catalyst, online conference, December 3, 2020.

20. "The State of Boys," MARC Summit by Catalyst.

21. "Cry Like a Man," video presentation delivered at the MARC Summit by Catalyst, online conference, December 3, 2020.

22. Denise Priest, "Working Fathers Really Need to Talk and Be Listened To," *The HR Director*, November 25, 2023, https://www.thehrdirector.com/business-news/mental-health/working-fathers-really-need-talk-listened.

23. Dan Witters, "U.S. Depression Rates Reach New Highs," *Good Morning America*, May 17, 2023; Mental Health America, "Let's Talk About Men's Mental Health," https://mhanational.org/harrys.

24. International Association for Suicide Prevention, *Global Suicide Statistics* (2021), https://www.iasp.info.

25. "Removing the Stigma of Men's Mental Health in the Workplace," panel discussion delivered at the MARC Summit hosted by Catalyst, online conference, December 3, 2020.

26. *Flexible Masculinities*, infographic (Catalyst).

27. *Mental Health at Work*, fact sheet (World Health Organization, 2024), https://www.who.int/news-room/fact-sheets/detail/mental-health-at-work.

28. Claire de Oliveira, Makeila Saka, Lauren Bone, and Rowena Jacobs, "The Role of Mental Health on Workplace Productivity: A Critical Review of the Literature," *Applied Health Economics and Health Policy* 21, no. 2 (2023): 167–93.
29. Brassel and Shaffer, *Most Men Support Gender Equity*.
30. "Removing the Stigma," MARC Summit by Catalyst.
31. David Taylor and Mike Wirth in conversation at the MARC Summit by Catalyst, online conference, December 3, 2020.
32. Brassel and Shaffer, *Most Men Support Gender Equity*.

Chapter 3

1. Kali Pal, Piaget, Zahidi, and Baller, *Global Gender Gap Report 2024*; *Women in Business 2025*; Hall, Laidlaw, Almtoft, Dhanasarnsombat, and Ramirez, "Women in Leadership."
2. *Actions Organizational Leaders Can Take to Build Advocates for Gender Equity*, infographic (Catalyst, 2021), last modified 2025, https://www.catalyst.org/insights/2021/actions-organizations-gender-equity; *Actions Employees at All Levels Can Take to Build Advocates for Gender Equity*, infographic (Catalyst, 2021), last modified 2025, https://www.catalyst.org/insights/2021/actions-individuals-gender-equity.
3. Shaffer, Sattari, and Pollack, *Interrupting Sexism at Work: How Men Respond*.
4. Andrea C. Vial, April H. Bailey, and John F. Dovidio, "People Who Accommodate Others' Sexist Views Are Themselves Perceived to Be Sexist," *Psychology of Women Quarterly* 48, no. 2 (2024): 252–70, https://doi.org/10.1177/03616843231221501.
5. Pollack and Kerr, *Engaging Men*.
6. Pollack and Kerr, *Engaging Men*.
7. Brassel and Shaffer, *Most Men Support Gender Equity*; Meg A. Warren, Samit D. Bordoloi, and Michael T. Warren, "Good for the Goose and Good for the Gander: Examining Positive Psychological Benefits of Male Allyship for Men and Women," *Psychology of Men & Masculinities* 22, no. 4 (2021): 723–31, https://doi.org/10.1037/men0000355.
8. Negin Sattari, Emily Shaffer, Sarah DiMuccio, and Dnika J. Travis, *Interrupting Sexism at Work: What Drives Men to Respond Directly or Do Nothing?* (Catalyst, 2020), https://www.catalyst.org/en-us/insights/2020/interrupting-sexism-workplace-men.

9. Dixon-Fyle, Huber, del Mar Martínez Márquez, Prince, Thomas, and Hunt, *Diversity Matters Even More*.

10. Travis, Shaffer, and Thorpe-Moscon, *Getting Real*.

11. Emilio J. Castilla and Stephen Benard, "The Paradox of Meritocracy in Organizations," *Administrative Science Quarterly* 55, no. 4 (2010): 543–676, https://doi.org/10.2189/asqu.2010.55.4.543.

12. Carter and Silva, *Myth of the Ideal Worker*.

13. Castilla and Benard, "The Paradox of Meritocracy."

14. Brassel and Shaffer, *Most Men Support Gender Equity*.

15. Sattari et al., *Interrupting Sexism at Work: What Drives Men to Respond*.

16. Shaffer, Sattari, and Pollack, *Interrupting Sexism at Work: How Men Respond*.

17. *Mad Men*, created by Matthew Weiner (Lionsgate Television, 2007–2015).

18. Manuela Barreto and David Matthew Boyle, "Benevolent and Hostile Sexism in a Shifting Global Context," *Nature Reviews Psychology* 2 (2023): 98–111, doi: 10.1038/s44159-022-00136-x.

19. Lilia M. Cortina, "Unseen Injustice: Incivility as Modern Discrimination in Organizations," *Academy of Management Review* 33, no. 1 (2008): 55–57, https://journals.aom.org/doi/10.5465/amr.2008.27745097.

20. Anthony G. Greenwald and Mahzarin R. Banaji, "Implicit Social Cognition: Attitudes, Self-Esteem, and Stereotypes," *Psychological Review* 102, no. 1 (1995): 4–27, doi: 10.1037/0033-295x.102.1.4; *What Are Implicit Associations?* infographic (Catalyst, 2025), https://www.catalyst.org/en-us/insights/2025/infographic-what-are-implicit-associations. Note that sexism intersects with other axes of inequalities and discriminations such as racism, ageism, and classism in shaping individual experiences and underprivileges.

21. *Flip the Script: Benevolent Sexism*, infographic (Catalyst, 2022), https://www.catalyst.org/en-us/insights/2022/benevolent-sexism-infographic; Barreto and Boyle, "Benevolent and Hostile Sexism."

22. Negin Sattari, Sarah H. DiMuccio, Joy Ohm, and Jose Romero, "Dismantling 'Benevolent' Sexism," *Harvard Business Review*, June 8, 2022, https://hbr.org/2022/06/dismantling-benevolent-sexism.

23. *Benevolent Sexism*, infographic (Catalyst); Peter Glick and Susan F. Fiske, "The Ambivalent Sexism Inventory: Differentiating Hostile and Benevolent Sexism," *Journal of Personality and Social Psychology* 70, no. 3 (1996): 491–512, https://psycnet.apa.org/doiLanding?doi=10.1037%2F0022-3514.70.3.491.

24. Kathleen Connelly and Martin Heesacker, "Why Is Benevolent Sexism Appealing? Associations with System Justification and Life Satisfaction,"

Psychology of Women Quarterly 36, no. 4 (2012): 432–443, https://doi.org/10
.1177/0361684312456369.

25. Rebecca Stewart, Brenna Wright, Liam Smith, Steven Roberts, and Natalie
Russell, "Gendered Stereotypes and Norms: A Systematic Review of Inter-
ventions Designed to Shift Attitudes and Behaviour," *Heliyon* 7, no. 4
(2021), doi: 10.1016/j.heliyon.2021.e06660.

26. "Author Talks: How Women Can Overcome the 'Broken Rung,'" McK-
insey & Company, January 24, 2025, https://www.mckinsey.com/featured
-insights/mckinsey-on-books/author-talks-how-women-can-overcome-the
-broken-rung.

27. Amy Diehl and Leanne M. Dzubinski, "How Biases About Motherhood
Impact All Women at Work," *Harvard Business Review*, July 30, 2024,
https://hbr.org/2024/07/how-biases-about-motherhood-impact-all-women
-at-work.

28. *Benevolent Sexism*, infographic (Catalyst).

29. Eden B. King, Whitney Botsford, Michelle R. Hebl, Stephanie Kazama,
Jeremy F. Dawson, and Andrew Perkins, "Benevolent Sexism at Work:
Gender Differences in the Distribution of Challenging Developmental
Experiences," *Journal of Management* 38, no. 6 (2012): 1835–66, https://doi
.org/10.1177/0149206310365902.

30. Joan C. Williams and Marina Multhaup, "For Women and Minorities to
Get Ahead, Managers Must Assign Work Fairly," *Harvard Business Review*,
March 5, 2018, https://hbr.org/2018/03/for-women-and-minorities-to-get
-ahead-managers-must-assign-work-fairly.

31. Sattari et al., *Interrupting Sexism at Work: What Drives Men to Respond.*

32. Sattari et al., *Interrupting Sexism at Work: What Drives Men to Respond.*

33. Sattari et al., *Interrupting Sexism at Work: What Drives Men to Respond.*

34. Sattari et al., *Interrupting Sexism at Work: What Drives Men to Respond.*

35. Sattari et al., *Interrupting Sexism at Work: What Drives Men to Respond.*

Chapter 4

1. Shaffer, Sattari, and Pollack, *Interrupting Sexism at Work: How Men Respond.*

2. Sattari et al., *Interrupting Sexism at Work: What Drives Men to Respond.*

3. Shaffer, Sattari, and Pollack, *Interrupting Sexism at Work: How Men Respond.*

4. Jennifer J. Kish-Gephart, James R. Detert, Linda Klebe Treviño, and Amy
C. Edmondson, "Silenced by Fear: The Nature, Sources, and Consequences

of Fear at Work," *Research in Organizational Behavior* 29 (2009): 163–93, https://doi.org/10.1016/j.riob.2009.07.002.

5. Maria Vakola and Dimitris Bouradas, "Antecedents and Consequences of Organisational Silence: An Empirical Investigation," *Employee Relations* 27, no. 5 (2015): 441–58, https://www.emerald.com/insight/content/doi/10.1108/01425450510611997/full/html.

6. Shaffer, Sattari, and Pollack, *Interrupting Sexism at Work: How Men Respond.*

7. Elizabeth Wolfe Morrison and Frances J. Milliken, "Organizational Silence: A Barrier to Change and Development in a Pluralistic World," *Academy of Management Review* 25, no. 4 (October, 2000): 706–25, https://doi.org/10.2307/259200.

8. Sonya Fontenot Premeaux and Arthur G. Bedeian, "Breaking the Silence: The Moderating Effects of Self-Monitoring in Predicting Speaking Up in the Workplace," *Journal of Management Studies* 40, no. 6 (2003): 1537–62, https://doi.org/10.1111/1467-6486.00390.

9. Sattari et al., *Interrupting Sexism at Work: What Drives Men to Respond.*

10. Shaffer, Sattari, and Pollack, *Interrupting Sexism at Work: How Men Respond.*

11. Sattari et al., *Interrupting Sexism at Work: What Drives Men to Respond.*

12. Robin J. Ely and Michael Kimmel, "Thoughts on the Workplace as a Masculinity Contest," *Journal of Social Issues* 74, no. 3 (2018): 628–634, doi:10.1111/josi.12290.

13. Berdahl et al., "Work as a Masculinity Contest."

14. Peter Glick, Jennifer L. Berdahl, and Natalya M. Alonso, "Development and Validation of the Masculinity Contest Culture Scale," *Journal of Social Issues* 74, no. 3 (September, 2018): 449–76, doi:10.1111/josi.12280; Natalya M. Alonso, "Playing to Win: Male-Male Sex-Based Harassment and the Masculinity Contest," *Journal of Social Issues* 74, no. 3 (September 2018): 477–99, https://doi.org/10.1111/josi.12283.

15. Sattari et al., *Interrupting Sexism at Work: What Drives Men to Respond.*

16. Brassel, *How to Reduce Gender-Based Hostility.*

17. Brassel, *How to Reduce Gender-Based Hostility.*

18. Sattari et al., *Interrupting Sexism at Work: What Drives Men to Respond*; James R. Detert, Ethan R. Burris, and David A. Harrison, "Do Your Employees Think Speaking Up Is Pointless?" *Harvard Business Review*, May 26, 2010, https://hbr.org/2010/05/do-your-employees-think-speaki; Elizabeth Wolfe Morrison, Sarah L. Wheeler-Smith, and Dishan Kamdar, "Speaking Up in Groups: A Cross-Level Study of Group Voice Climate and Voice," *Journal of Applied Psychology* 96, no. 1 (2011): 183–91, doi:10.1037/a0020744.

19. Sattari et al., *Interrupting Sexism at Work: What Drives Men to Respond.*

20. Sattari et al., *Interrupting Sexism at Work: What Drives Men to Respond.*

21. Detert, Burris, and Harrison, *Do Your Employees Think.*

Chapter 5

1. Travis, Shaffer, and Thorpe-Moscon, *Getting Real.*

2. Yellen, "History of Women's Work."

3. "Equal Pay Act," History.com, accessed June 12, 2025, https://www.history.com/articles/equal-pay-act.

4. Brassel and Shaffer, *Most Men Support Gender Equity*; Promundo, *So, You Want to Be a Male Ally for Gender Equality? (And You Should): Results from a National Survey, and a Few Things You Should Know* (Promundo, 2019).

5. *What Is Gender Partnership and How to Be an Effective Gender Partner*, infographic (Catalyst, 2023), https://www.catalyst.org/en-us/insights/2023/gender-partnership-infographic.

6. Sarah DiMuccio et al., *Gender Partnership: What, Why, How* (Catalyst, 2022), https://www.catalyst.org/insights/2022/gender-equity-partnership-tool.

7. "Our Vision," White Men for Racial Justice (WMRJ.org), accessed June 18, 2025, https://www.wmrj.org.

8. Jeanine Prime and Corinne A. Moss-Racusin, *Engaging Men in Gender Initiatives: What Change Agents Need to Know* (Catalyst, 2009), https://www.catalyst.org/insights/2009/engaging-men-gender-initiatives-change.

9. *Women in the Workplace 2021* (LeanIn.org and McKinsey & Company).

10. Negin Sattari, Sarah DiMuccio, and Ludo Gabriele, *When Managers Are Open, Men Feel Heard and Interrupt Sexism* (Catalyst, 2021), https://www.catalyst.org/insights/2021/managers-openness-sexism.

11. *Men Who Feel Their Manager Is Open and That Their Voice Is Heard Are More Likely to Interrupt Sexism* (Catalyst, 2021), https://www.catalyst.org/about/newsroom/2021/manager-openness-men-interrupting-sexism.

12. "Dow CEO: Coming Out Made Me a More Inclusive Leader," Catalyst, 2021, https://www.catalyst.org/en-us/insights/2021/dow-ceo-jim-fitterling-coming-out-workplace-inclusion.

13. Christian Conti, LinkedIn posts, September 17, 2024, and November 11, 2024. GARTNER is a registered trademark and service mark of Gartner,

Chapter 6

1. *Women in the Workplace 2024* (McKinsey & Company and Leanin.org).
2. *Flexible Masculinities*, infographic (Catalyst).
3. Clay Risen, "Frank Shrontz, 92, Dies; Led Boeing in the Last of Its Golden Years," *The New York Times*, May 22, 2024, https://www.nytimes.com/2024/05/22/business/frank-shrontz-dead.html.
4. Alan Mulally, "Working Together Leadership & Management System," Presentation in *Love in Action*, podcast episode titled "Transform Your Organization with Alan Mulally's 'Working Together' System," December 18, 2024, 1:26:51, https://www.marcelschwantes.com/transform-your-organization-with-alan-mulallys-working-together-system-ep-234.
5. *Implicit Associations*, infographic (Catalyst).
6. "Managing Affinity Bias: Knowledge Burst," Catalyst, 2019, https://www.catalyst.org/insights/2025/managing-affinity-bias.
7. *Implicit Associations*, infographic (Catalyst).
8. *Implicit Associations*, infographic (Catalyst); "Managing Affinity Bias," Catalyst; *Break the Cycle—Eliminating Gender Bias in Talent Management Systems*, infographic (Catalyst, 2018), last modified 2025, https://www.catalyst.org/en-us/insights/2018/break-the-cycle-eliminating-gender-bias-in-talent-management-system.
9. "11 Harmful Types of Unconscious Bias and How to Interrupt Them," Catalyst, 2020, https://www.catalyst.org/en-us/insights/2020/interrupt-unconscious-bias.

Chapter 7

1. Pollack and Kerr, *Engaging Men*.
2. Claire Cain Miller, "Fathers Gained Family Time in the Pandemic. Many Don't Want to Give It Back," *The New York Times*, March 12, 2023, https://www.nytimes.com/2023/03/12/upshot/fathers-pandemic-remote-work.html.

3. *Modern Mobility: Moving Women with Purpose* (PwC, 2016), https://www.pwc.com/gr/en/publications/assets/modern-mobility-moving-women-with-purpose.pdf.

4. *INtersections 2023 Progress Report: Advancing Our Ambition* (Dow Inc., 2023), https://investors.dow.com/en/news/news-details/2024/Dow-releases-2023-INtersections-Report-outlining-progress-toward-its-sustainability-commitments/default.aspx.

5. Nuala Walsh, "How to Encourage Employees to Speak Up When They See Wrongdoing," *Harvard Business Review*, February 4, 2021, https://hbr.org/2021/02/how-to-encourage-employees-to-speak-up-when-they-see-wrongdoing.

6. Aviroop Biswas, Shireen Harbin, Emma Irvin, Heather Johnston, Momtaz Begum, Margaret Tiong, et al., "Sex and Gender Differences in Occupational Hazard Exposures: A Scoping Review of the Recent Literature," *Current Environmental Health Reports* 8, no. 4 (2021): 267–80, doi: 10.1007/s40572-021-00330-8.

7. Travis, Shaffer, and Thorpe-Moscon, *Getting Real.*

8. Warren, Bordoloi, and Warren, "Good for the Goose."

Chapter 8

1. Yang Yang, Tanya Y. Tian, Teresa K. Woodruff, Benjamin F. Jones, and Brian Uzzi, "Gender-Diverse Teams Produce More Novel and Higher-Impact Scientific Ideas," *Proceedings of the National Academy of Sciences of the United States of America* 119 (no. 36), e2200841119.

2. Laura Sherbin and Ripa Rashid, "Diversity Doesn't Stick Without Inclusion," *Harvard Business Review*, February 1, 2017, https://hbr.org/2017/02/diversity-doesnt-stick-without-inclusion.

3. *Catalyst Sponsorship Guide: Why Sponsorship Programs Are Important* (Catalyst, 2025), https://www.catalyst.org/insights/2025/catalyst-sponsorship-guide.

4. Bonita Thompson, "How Leaders Develop Collaborative Leadership for Effectiveness" (PhD diss., University of Pennsylvania, 2022).

5. Janice Gassam Asare, "4 Ways to Build Your Company's Diverse Pipeline," *Forbes*, July 24, 2019, https://www.forbes.com/sites/janicegassam/2019/07/24/4-ways-to-build-your-companys-diverse-pipeline.

6. *Catalyst Guide to Employee Resource Groups (ERGs)* (Catalyst, 2025); Natacha Catalino, Nora Gardner, Drew Goldstein, and Jackie Wong, "Effective Employee Resource Groups Are Key to Inclusion at Work. Here's How to Get Them Right," McKinsey & Company, December 7, 2022, https://www.mckinsey.com/capabilities/people-and-organizational-performance/our-insights/effective-employee-resource-groups-are-key-to-inclusion-at-work-heres-how-to-get-them-right.

7. "Working at Dow," Great Place to Work, 2025, https://www.greatplacetowork.com/certified-company/1000265.

8. DiMuccio et al., *Gender Partnership*.

9. Travis, Shaffer, and Thorpe-Moscon, *Getting Real*.

10. Travis, Shaffer, and Thorpe-Moscon, *Getting Real*.

11. Henrik Bresman and Amy C. Edmondson, "Research: To Excel, Diverse Teams Need Psychological Safety," *Harvard Business Review*, March 17, 2022, https://hbr.org/2022/03/research-to-excel-diverse-teams-need-psychological-safety.

12. Travis, Shaffer, and Thorpe-Moscon, *Getting Real*.

13. "Dow CEO," Catalyst.

Chapter 9

1. Sattari et al., *Interrupting Sexism at Work: What Drives Men to Respond*.

2. Sheila Brassel, Tara Van Bommel, and Lauren Pasquarella Daley, *Why Empathy Is a Superpower in the Future of Work* (Catalyst, 2020), https://www.catalyst.org/en-us/insights/2020/empathy-superpower-future-of-work.

3. Tara Van Bommel, *The Power of Empathy in Times of Crisis and Beyond* (Catalyst, 2021), last modified 2025, https://www.catalyst.org/en-us/insights/2025/empathy-work-strategy-crisis.

4. Costigan, *The Double-Bind*.

5. Brassel, Van Bommel, and Daley, *Why Empathy Is a Superpower*; Van Bommel, *The Power of Empathy*.

6. Van Bommel, *The Power of Empathy*.

7. Peter Sear, "3 Consequences of a Lack of Empathy in Leadership," *Psychology Today*, March 9, 2021, https://www.psychologytoday.com/us/blog/empathic-minds/202103/3-consequences-lack-empathy-in-leadership.

8. Van Bommel, *The Power of Empathy*.

9. "Catalyst Elevates Empathy as Business Skill This International Women's Day," Catalyst (press release), March 1, 2022, https://www.prnewswire.com/news-releases/catalyst-elevates-empathy-as-business-skill-this-international-womens-day-301492281.html.

10. *Flexible Masculinities*, infographic (Catalyst).

11. Brassel and Shaffer, *Most Men Support Gender Equity*.

12. Brassel, *How to Reduce Gender-Based Hostility*.

13. DiMuccio et al., *Gender Partnership: What, Why, How*.

14. "11 Harmful Types," Catalyst.

15. "Chobani Founder & CEO on Putting Humanity First," Catalyst, May 9, 2021, https://www.catalyst.org/insights/2021/chobani-hamdi-ulukaya-diversity-equity-inclusion.

16. *ERG Leader's Guide to Gender Partnership* (Catalyst, 2024).

17. Brassel and Ramos, *Intersectionality: When Identities Converge*.

18. Sheila Brassel, Emily Shaffer, and Dnika J. Travis, *Emotional Tax and Work Teams: A View from 5 Countries* (Catalyst, 2022), https://www.catalyst.org/en-us/insights/2022/emotional-tax-teams.

19. Brassel and Ramos, *Intersectionality: When Identities Converge*; Emily Shaffer and Heather Foust-Cummings, *Build Belonging by Focusing on Inclusion* (Catalyst, 2024), https://www.catalyst.org/insights/2024/build-belonging-with-inclusion; Sheila Brassel, Joy Ohm, and Dnika J. Travis, *Allyship and Curiosity Drive Inclusion for People of Color at Work* (Catalyst, 2021), https://www.catalyst.org/insights/2021/allyship-curiosity-employees-of-color.

20. DiMuccio et al., *Gender Partnership: What, Why, How*.

21. Ashir Coillberg, "A Window into the Wage Gap: What's Behind It and How to Close It," *National Women's Law Center*, February 2025, https://nwlc.org/wp-content/uploads/2025/02/2025-Window-Into-the-Wage-Gap-Factsheet.pdf.

22. Corin Ramos, "Why Intersectionality Matters," Catalyst, 2020, https://www.catalyst.org/en-us/insights/2020/intersectionality-workplace-2020.

23. Dnika J. Travis and Jennifer Thorpe-Moscon, *Day-to-Day Experiences of Emotional Tax Among Women and Men of Color in the Workplace* (Catalyst, 2018), https://www.nigp.org/forum/pre-reads/Day-To-Day-Experiences-of-Emotional-Tax-Among-Women-and-Men-of-Color-in-the-Workplace.pdf; Jennifer Thorpe-Moscon, Alixandra Pollack, and Olufemi Olu-Lafe, *Empowering Workplaces Combat Emotional Tax for People of Colour in*

Canada (Catalyst, 2019), https://www.nlc.bc.ca/wp-content/uploads/2024
/03/Empowering-Workplaces-to-Combat-Emotional-Tax-for-People-of
-Colour.pdf; Jennifer Thorpe-Moscon and Joy Ohm, *Building Inclusion for
Indigenous Peoples in Canadian Workplaces* (Catalyst, 2021), https://www
.catalyst.org/en-us/insights/2021/inclusion-indigenous-peoples-canada
-workplace; Sheila Brassel, Emily Shaffer, and Dnika J. Travis, *Emotional
Tax and Work Teams: A View from 5 Countries* (Catalyst, 2022), https://www
.catalyst.org/en-us/insights/2022/emotional-tax-teams.

24. Travis, Shaffer, and Thorpe-Moscon, *Getting Real.*

25. Doug Flaig, "How Leaders Can Model Work-Life Balance," *Forbes*, January 3, 2024, https://www.forbes.com/councils/forbesbusinesscouncil/2024
/01/03/how-leaders-can-model-work-life-balance.

26. Van Bommel, *The Power of Empathy*; Travis, Shaffer, and Thorpe-Moscon,
Getting Real.

Conclusion

1. Pollack, Glasgow, Van Bommel, Joseph, and Yoshino, *Risks of Retreat.*

2. *Evolving Together: Flourishing in the Age-Diverse Workforce* (BSI, 2024); Richard Fry and Dana Braga, *Older Workers Are Growing in Number and Earning Higher Wages* (Pew Research Center, 2023), https://www.pewresearch
.org/social-trends/2023/12/14/older-workers-are-growing-in-number-and
-earning-higher-wages.

3. "Labor Force Participation Rate, Female (% of Female Population Ages 15+) (Modeled ILO Estimate)," World Bank Group, 2025, https://data
.worldbank.org/indicator/SL.TLF.ACTI.FE.ZS; "Labor Force Statistics from the Current Population Survey: Women in the Labor Force," US Bureau of Labor Statistics, 2024, https://www.bls.gov/cps/demographics
/women-labor-force.htm.

4. Hurst, "U.S. Women Are Outpacing."

5. "Wise Up to Women," Nielsen, 2020, https://www.nielsen.com/insights
/2020/wise-up-to-women.

6. Edward Helmore, "Gen Z Will Be Last Generation with White Majority in US, Study Finds," *The Guardian*, August 8, 2023, https://www.theguardian
.com/profile/edwardhelmore/2023/aug/08/all.

7. Travis, Shaffer, and Thorpe-Moscon, *Getting Real*; Shaffer and Foust-Cummings, *Build Belonging*.

8. Travis, Shaffer, and Thorpe-Moscon, *Getting Real*; Van Bommel, *The Power of Empathy*; "Why Diversity and Inclusion Matter," Catalyst.

9. Jean M. Twenge, "How Gen Z Changed Its Views on Gender," *Time*, May 1, 2023, https://time.com/6275663/generation-z-gender-identity.

10. Adam Stanaland, "Mark Zuckerberg Thinks Workplaces Need to 'Man Up'—Here's Why That's Bad for All Employees, No Matter Their Gender," *The Conversation*, January 23, 2025, https://theconversation.com/mark-zuckerberg-thinks-workplaces-need-to-man-up-heres-why-thats-bad-for-all-employees-no-matter-their-gender-247539.

11. Brassel and Shaffer, *Most Men Support Gender Equity*.

Appendix

1. *Getting to Know MARC* (Catalyst, 2021), updated 2025, https://www.catalyst.org/insights/2021/getting-to-know-marc.

INDEX

ABOUT THE AUTHOR

 Jennifer McCollum is a recognized global leadership expert, speaker, author, and CEO committed to building inclusive workplaces by accelerating progress for women and engaging men as partners in change. She currently serves as President and CEO of Catalyst, a global non-profit that has been at the forefront of women's advancement and inclusion since the 1960s. Today, Catalyst accelerates organizational performance and women's progress through original research, convenings, tools, and support that enable organizations to make inclusion a business practice at scale.

Her first book, *In Her Own Voice: A Woman's Rise to CEO*, became an Amazon bestseller and offered women practical strategies to overcome barriers on the path to leadership. With her second book, she expands the conversation, equipping leaders with insights and tools to break free from outdated norms and build cultures of partnership that help leaders, teams, and organizations succeed.

Previously, Jennifer was the first female CEO of Linkage, a leadership development firm focused on changing the face of leadership, where she successfully led its acquisition by SHRM (the Society for Human Resource Management).

Her insights have appeared in *The Wall Street Journal*, *Fast Company*, *Forbes*, *Reuters*, and *Fortune*, and she has spoken on hundreds of stages worldwide.

An avid tennis player and skier, Jennifer is also the mother of three and lives in the Washington, DC, area with her husband.

ABOUT CATALYST

Catalyst is a global nonprofit that has been the recognized expert at the forefront of women's advancement and inclusion since the 1960s.

Today, Catalyst accelerates organizational performance and women's progress through research-backed insights, high-impact convenings, proven solutions, and unparalleled support that fuel organizations to make inclusion a business practice at scale.

Catalyst is a 501(c)(3) tax-exempt organization.

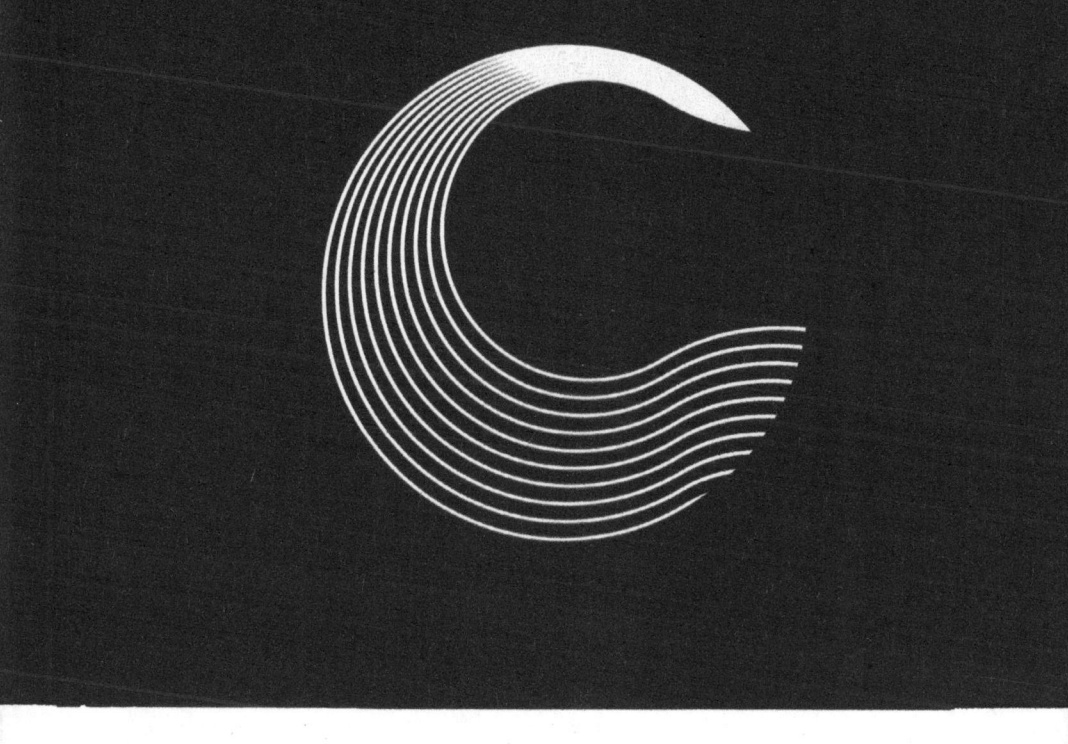

Turn insight into impact.

You've explored the roadmap—now drive change.
Catalyst can help your teams put gender partnership into action.

Explore our learning solutions.
Book a speaking engagement with Jennifer.
Download your book club kit.

Start moving from ideas to implementation.
Visit www.catalyst.org/men-at-work

CATALYST